Green Business, Green Values, and Sustainability

Routledge Studies in Corporate Governance

Contents

Illustrations

1 CIBAM and the Symposium on "Green Business and Green Values"

Christos N. Pitelis

INTRODUCTION

The aim of this chapter is to introduce the reader to the nature and philosophy of the Center for International Business & Management (CIBAM) and zero in on one of its major functions, the Symposium, in particular the one in February 2009 on "Green Business and Green Values." In addition, we summarize the main points made at the introductory talk by the Director of CIBAM (the present author). A short summary of all the proceedings, to include some of the discussion, appears after the introduction—signed by a group of Cambridge MBAs who attended the Symposium and co-authored the report. Here, I will only refer to the topics covered, the authors and rationale, as well as to the articles included in this book.

CIBAM AND THE CIBAM GLOBAL BUSINESS SYMPOSIA

CIBAM's Identity and History

CIBAM is a research center established in 1995 within the Judge Business School, at the University of Cambridge. It is the oldest such center. It was co-founded by Professor John Child and the present author, with John Child serving as the first Founding Director, from 1995 to 1997. The present author, who was then Associate Director, took over as a Director of CIBAM in 1997. Noreena Hertz was appointed Associate Director. An inaugural meeting-mini conference took place to mark this in July 1997 at St. John's College, Cambridge, attended by friends—academics and business leaders, the last mentioned invited to join as advisory board members. Founding Board Members included Sir Martin Sorrell, CEO WPP; Mr. Jack Keenan, then CEO of the United Distillers and Vintners; Mr. Manfred Tuerks, Managing Director, AT Kearney, Automotives; and Marc Verstringhe, then CEO of Catering and Allied.

Following presentations by some academics on issues they felt might interest the business people present, the discussion zeroed in on what should be the nature, philosophy and function of CIBAM, to include the interactions and divisions of tasks between the academics and business people.

The role of research centers within business schools is not as easy to determine as in some other schools, for example mathematics or engineering. The aim of the theoretical mathematician, for example, is to come up with fundamental research output that may or may not be of commercial relevance. In an engineering or physics department, on the other hand, research to output is normally expected to have clear, discernible commercial applications. Business schools stand somewhere in between. The research output of a business school is normally expected to be simultaneously rigorous and with clear implications to managerial practice, albeit without necessary commercial applications. It is, so to speak, high-brow potential prescription. Clearly the above description does not apply to all business schools, or the other types of schools mentioned, but this is a usual expectation.

When originally conceived by John Child as a Center for International Management, the intention was to focus on research issues pertaining to the management of international business, particularly multinational enterprises (MNEs), what we call in academic circles International Management (IM). John Child, who moved to Birmingham University in 1997, is a global leader in this field. IM deals with issues pertaining to the "insides" of MNEs, for example their internal organizational structure; the link between structure, strategy and performance, the way through which MNEs can leverage the skills of their subsidiaries, the role of autonomy versus control of subsidiaries; how MNEs can deal with issues of organizational coordination and communication, whether and how to adapt to local taste in "host" countries, or to aim for cost reductions through integration. Issues of culture and inter-cultural management are critical in this context, as they are the particularities of IM in emerging markets, such as China, East Asia, Russia, India, Brazil and now Africa. Some of the founding academic members of CIBAM, notably Noreena Hertz, Malcolm Warner and Charles Hampden-Turner, had unique knowledge and competence on these issues, rendering these a natural original focus of CIBAM's research.

Another aspect of International Business (IB) scholarship, as for example practiced by associations such as the Academy of International Business (AIB), and its European, regional and national counterparts, for example the European International Business Association (EIBA), focus also on the issues pertaining to the nature, objectives, growth, boundaries and strategies of MNEs and the impact of the above on MNE performance. Focal issues here include the choice of modality by MNEs (e.g., foreign direct investment versus licencing/franchising, and inter-firm cooperation, such as joint ventures and strategic alliances); how being an MNE can help firms capture value from their advantages (whether through efficiency, market power or a combination); the interactions between MNEs, regions and nations; the competitiveness of firms, regions and nations; government policies toward MNEs, to include trade, foreign direct investment (FDI), and cluster and other microeconomic and macroeconomic policies that can have an impact on MNE decisions. These aspects of IB are based more on business economics and international political economy (IPE) foundations. They are closely linked to IM concerns (e.g., a badly implemented entry through FDI will lead to failure, even if FDI was the best entry modality theoretically), and they also involve their special considerations. These aspects of IB were the research focus of the present author, who moreover was working at that time on the supply-side (industrial) and catching-up strategies of East Asian countries, such as Japan and the Four Tigers (Hong Kong, Singapore, Korea, Taiwan)—including their attributes and policies towards FDI and MNEs—and compared them to Western policies, and those of the emerging Central and Eastern European "transition" economies. Noreena Hertz, too, was working on international competitiveness issues, in general and particularly in Russia, where she had done work with Michael Porter. Peter Nolan, a founding academic member, was carrying out research on the "global business revolution" in general, and with particular reference to China, on which he is one of the leading Western experts.

The complementarities, both conceptual and regional, were far too obvious for John Child to miss, and following a discussion with the present author the two agreed to create a center with a BA between the CI and the M—leading to CIBAM. The research focus of the center, as a natural result would be:

• The nature, growth, boundaries and strategies of MNEs, to include entry modalities, such as FDI, franchising and joint ventures;
• The competitiveness of firms, regions and nations and government policies toward FDI and MNEs;
• The management of MNEs to include inter-cultural management issues;
• The particularities and comparative analysis of emerging economies, notably China, East Asia, Russia, Central and Eastern Europe vis-à-vis mainly IM, but also IB-related concerns.

Identifying the focus, joint interests and complementarities, and aiming to undertake collaborative research, and research-related activities by building critical mass, is by itself an important enough reason to set up and maintain a research center within a business school—provided the quality of the people and their research interests and focus are sufficiently rigorous and business relevant. But CIBAM was faced with a more specific challenge. At the inaugural meeting in St John's and after having attended my presentation, Sir Martin simply asked, "and what is in it for me?" This led to the appreciation that thinking one is doing business-relevant research is not enough; research needs to also be perceived as relevant by business. One way to do this is by developing tools (such as Michael Porter's five-forces model) which distill the essence of academic research but target it specifically to business policy makers. This involves elements of both research and consulting. However, it does remain at arm's length, so to speak. The academic does the work, and he or she teaches it to, or consults, the business.

While there is nothing wrong with the above, and members of CIBAM certainly do this too, there was and still is debate in business school circles of the need for deeper interaction between business and academia, with each party contributing where they possess comparative advantage and each getting what they need from this collaboration. Starting from the objectives, both business and academics (as well as firms and indeed regions and nations) share one objective in common: to capture value out of their perceived to be value creating and appropriable advantages. What differs is not so much the generic objective, but the metrics—what is being measured. Businesses focus on the bottom line (profit), hopefully subject to this being sustainable for them and the wider community, and they have subsidiary interests on philosophical-academic issues and research, usually to the extent it helps them leverage it for commercial purposes. Academics in business schools aim for maximum impact through rigorous and relevant top-quality research, published in scholarly journals, subject to making a good living out of this activity, in terms of salary and consulting. Wider, societal concerns are often (albeit not always, or perhaps as much as they should) part and parcel of business school research: for example current debates on Corporate Social Responsibility (CSR) and Business Ethics.

One way through which the mutual interests of both parties can be satisfied is by convening high-level events (call them colloquia, symposia, conferences) where the two parties physically meet and exchange ideas on a theme of business relevance. This is not consulting per se; it is not business-funded research either. Instead, it is a genuine two-way street in which both parties give and take. Academics give state-of-the-art knowledge and rigor. Business provides topicality, immediacy, and foresight. As regards business-relevant research, for example, it is difficult for an academic to be aware of current and emerging (especially immediate) concerns of business. In this context, business academics can get inside knowledge and insight on what are also likely business concerns of the present and near future. For example, at a time when for the present author, declining (but still at around 7%) unemployment seemed to be an economic concern, Sir Martin Sorrell suggested that "talent wars" (the attempt by business to acquire talent) was the critical issue for his business. That led to the fourth (July 2001) symposium, "Talent Wars . . . Why and How to Compete."

In addition to possessing more time for research, academics also possess conceptual frameworks that can serve as a lens through which one can analyze, propose solutions and even attempt to predict longer-term trends. Now business academics and economists are notoriously bad of predicting anything in particular with much success, but there are various cases where a decent conceptual framework afforded impressive predictions. An example is the father figure of IB, Stephen Hymer, who, back in the early 1970s, predicted the far more recent trend toward outsourcing (see Cohen et al., 1979), by analyzing the respective disadvantages of integration versus outsourcing and proposing that firms would gradually aim to keep the advantages of both, by removing the disadvantages of outsourcing (the lack of control) by developing brands and maintaining the control of "intangibles" and some tangibles (e.g., the Coca-Cola secret recipe). There are more such examples suggesting that business academics too can be of further value to business.

Ideas such as the above led to the adoption of the Forum; initially named Colloquium, it was subsequently renamed as Symposium (from Plato's homonymous book) to reflect the fact that the meetings involved not just the interactions of ideas but also the consumption of food and drink, which is far closer to the etymology of the "Symposium" (literally drinking together, from *syn* = "together" and *pinein* = "drinking"!). Indeed, there has been lots of drinking and eating since.

Based on the idea that businesses know better what they need to know (an almost tautological statement, yet not necessarily always true, especially on longer-term sustainability-related issues), the decision was for the global advisory board to determine at a board meeting the topics of the Symposia. The result was a resounding success and also rather surprising. It was surprising because some of the issues selected (e.g., "Ageing" or "Religion") did not quite strike, originally at least, as being too business-related— rather they looked quite academic, not at least to this author. A resounding success, not least because almost invariably the topics were selected well before (often up to two years) the Symposium, the topics became headline news at just about Symposium time. The Global Financial Crisis Symposium in February 2008 could not be a better example. When the topic was proposed by CIBAM board member Jonathan Garner (managing director, Morgan Stanley), the only interest anyone had on financial markets was how to make more money out of the relentless and apparently endless rally of stocks and house prices. Jonathan instead was seeing clouds—a bear, I thought, albeit he did not appear like one. Two years later, the crisis almost coincided with the Symposium; it was hard to find speakers as some were losing, or moving, jobs; and there was some excitement, concern and, dare I say, panic. Now, economists should be able to predict this (the conceptual lens is definitely there), but few dared—perhaps it is the fear of reputational loss. Jonathan did. This almost spooky predictive capability of the board became a major reason for the success of the events. Others include the venue, the format, the participants—in short the "business model and the "value proposition."

Much of the above is an evolutionary, learning, trial-and-error process. The first few meetings were one-day events, but soon we moved to a two-day event involving one night stay in Cambridge, starting Friday afternoon and ending Saturday evening with the board meeting. From 2005 we decided to move it to start Thursday evening and finish Friday evening—all in 24 hours, from 5:00 p.m. on Thursday to 5:00 p.m. on Friday, followed by the board meeting.

Concerning the format, early events involved few (four or five) stand-up talks, mainly by academics followed by some questions—admittedly a rather tedious experience for people traveling from abroad for the purpose. Through a continuous process of learning and (mostly) improvement, the final product involves as many as 15 to 20 speakers, panelists, chairs and discussants, over the 24 hours. There are now panels, as well as stand-up lectures. Speakers are allowed to talk for around half of their allocated time (40 minutes for stand-up speakers, 10 to 15 minutes per panellist), followed by very intensive and often heated debate.

Speakers involve a mix of around 50–70% business people and practitioners (normally however with impressive academic credentials), around 30% academics and up to 20% policymakers or students, normally chosen from the current Cambridge MBA class and some MBA alumni. All these are carefully selected from a much wider link of potential speakers, created mainly through the Network (the CIBAM members and friends) but also through in-house research.

As the critical element of success is the dialogue and the exchange of ideas, the number of participants is capped to a maximum of between 55 and 70, the usual number. From these around 30 are business people, 15 to 20 are academics, and up to 15 are MBA students and guests. The MBA students are selected on the basis of background and interest in the topic, and they are asked to help produce a report from the proceedings, such as the one that follows this introduction.

In the early days the venue was a Cambridge College—preferably a different one each time. Following the completion of the new Judge Business School building, the Thursday part takes place in a College and the Friday, at the Judge. On Thursday evening there is a gala dinner at the College—usually in one of the Grand Old Halls. Gradually there emerged the institution of informal drinks at the lobby bar of a Cambridge hotel by the river. This turned out to involve lots of it, I am afraid some times up to 5:00 a.m. (with the Symposium recommencing at 9:00 a.m., usually proceeded by breakfast at the hotel, at around 8!) In the bad old days, there was also a fair amount of cigars, but this is now regarded as a terrorist act (at least indoors)!

In addition to the Symposium, we gradually developed the CIBAM Distinguished Lecture series, usually once a year, lately combined with a panel. The initial effort was to have this delivered by women, as a means of levelling the playing field, and mainly because so many excellent ones can sometimes be bypassed by equally deserving men. Noreena Hertz (2001), Vicky Pryce (2002), and Dame Sandra Dawson (2004) gave some of the early lectures. Gradually, we gave in to bringing in men (mostly for expediency and the provision of more choice). David Teece (2006), Pankaj Ghemawat (2007), former Prime Minister of Greece Costas Simitis (2008) and Alain Verbeke (2009) gave these lectures. These are now also on a Thursday evening and are followed by the usual gala dinner in a Cambridge College—and the "informal drinks," too (but thankfully with more than a three-hour sleep time before Friday morning!).

The Cambridge-base of the Symposia (in effect the contribution of the ingredients described above) proved a successful one. Attempts to move out (e.g., an event took place at the WPP headquarters in London, hosted by Sir Martin Sorrell) were not quite the same. On the other hand, the Symposium on Southeastern Europe in Athens (2009) was a remarkable success. So it is not easy to generalize. We often debate about this, not least, for example, as to why some extremely busy people will almost invariably make time to come from places such as the United States, Russia and Taiwan. It would appear that the Cambridge experience (being cut off, away from it all), the concentrated intensive knowledge exchange over the 24 hours, and, of course, meeting up with old friends and a possible weekend break, all contribute. Whatever it is, it seems to work.

This is also evidenced by many requests for knowledge transfer both within Cambridge and internationally. For example, a variant of the Symposium format was tried in St. Petersburg, where the author was visiting in 2007; the CIBAM model was also used at the Center for International Business and Innovation (CIBI) in Copenhagen Business School, with the present author, as one of the two keynote speakers, discussing the CIBAM experience.

Other CIBAM events include an internal seminar series at the Judge. Other activities involve mainly selected research projects.

Research output has been of three main types. One is the CIBAM members' own research, which benefits from the interaction with the business community by getting some inside knowledge as to what currently matters for business. The present author, for example, regularly to issues or ideas discussed at the Symposia in his papers. A second type involves CIBAM-sponsored books and case studies; examples are the book detailing the history of Catering and Allied and the case study on the Advanced Management Program International (AMPI), which was the first attempt to transfer to the UK the Harvard experience, led by Harvard Professor Harry Hansen. As a result the subsequently created Harry Hansen Trust decided to continue its activities in collaboration with CIBAM. A third type of output involves the proceedings of the events. These are published as a CIBAM book (such as the present one), in journals and, when possible, as special issue of journals. Such special issues included in the past Business Ethics, Corporate Governance and Global Business and Economics Review. The present book is another example. Other papers from Symposia presentations have been published in journals such as Contributions to Political Economy. Collaborations, between CIBAM members resulted in publications in the Journal of International Business Studies (see Dunning and Pitelis, 2008) and Organization Science (see Mahoney et al., 2009). Particularly striking has been the success of the Corporate Governance special issue. The model (to include academic articles and articles by business leaders, NGOs and activists) was a major success. A number of the ten most cited articles from the journal were for some time from this special issue, the one by Jack Keenan (CIBAM patron) was the second most cited article. The article itself was a short account of Jack's own personal experience from boardrooms. Nothing very academic at all—it looks like there is a need for more of that in business scholarship.

Membership

An organization is as good as its members. At CIBAM we have been privileged. Cambridge is an attractive place, with special people. This helps attract more special people. Over time we were privileged to create a network of business leaders, academics and some policymakers, all of the highest standing. Membership (and its type), much like everything else, evolved. We started with a few intra-Judge academics and founding board business members. At the time of writing this, there are four major categories: global advisory board members, business associates, academic advisory board members and Cambridge-based academics. The management mainly includes the present author, the associate director, one research assistant and one administrative assistant. Others, like our external liaisons person (M. Vintiadis) and our academic advisory board, help and advise, as much as they are able to, given the non-stipendary nature of the positions.

Critical for CIBAM's progress has been its first expansion phase that took place in 1998–2000. That was mostly the result of the effort of CIBAM's associate director Noreena Hertz. Noreena undertook the task to prepare a value proposition, select possible board members, approach them and invite them to apply to join the board. That led to some remarkable additions to our board, such as Len Blavatnik, Jean-Michel Broun, Tommy Helsby, Andrew Morgan and Vicky Pryce. For reasons to soon become clear, CIBAM as it is now, would not be without this effort. We owe a big thanks to Dame Sandra Dawson (then director of the Judge), who helped, by waiving Judge overheads and liaising with and helping Noreena.

The academic advisory board was intentionally left rather small, and quite exclusive. Currently it includes Peter Buckley, John Child and David Teece, all known enough not to require further comment. The academic associates include selected leading academics from other universities. The business associates are leading business people, albeit with less involvement on the decision-making process, an issue to which I return. At the moment overall membership exceeds 100 people, from many countries and continents, from all types of business and from many top academic institutions. The full list of current CIBAM members can be found in Appendix I of this introduction.

Drawing on the joint expertise of such a network for potential speakers and other Symposium participants is a blessing. Combined with the remarkable foresight of our board, that selects the Symposia topics, we were privileged to deal with issues such as "Russia 2008—Putin's Legacy to his Successor" (back in 2004!). The issues of ethics, talent wars, ageing, environmental sustainability, corporate governance, religion, media, and security, terrorism and business were all remarkably topical and exciting events. Just indicatively the event on media coincided with the publication of cartoons offensive to the Islamic religion, the one on corporate governance was decided before, and took place soon after the Enron scandals. I find it hard to believe that this could have happened, were it not for the nose and instinct of those on the ground (the business people), who both sense such developments and have the high-power incentive to do something as they feel their impact on their bottom line—current and emerging. Quite often (but not always) the comments from the participants and the board were that "that was the best Symposium yet!"

In addition to selecting the topics, helping to propose and bring in speakers (usually in the form of an organizing committee of two or three who proposed the topic and had special knowledge of, and interest in, it), and getting involved themselves as speakers, panelists, chairs, or just a critical audience with astute questions, the function of the board at the board meetings is to provide feedback and suggestions for improvement— on the speakers, the format, the composition, the context, the venues, everything pertaining to the Symposium. Most important, however, is the strategic role—what we want to be; where are we heading; what we want to do next. These are not easy issues, and there is often heated debate. For example, a recurrent theme is whether we should remain an exclusive "boutique" or aim to expand, with an eye to possibly becoming a mini-Davos, but with a specific theme/focus for each meeting, as well on other different features such as more intimacy and perhaps a more "critical" focus in the sense of being cognisant of the need to deal with globalization's potentially negative "externalities."

Such debates help us sharpen our understanding of what we are, what we try to do and why. I believe that through an evolutionary process, there is now at least an implicit understanding of the idea that we aim to explore the interrelationship between practice, theory and policy, with an eye to prescribing better policy and practice, for business firms, but also governments and more widely (e.g., international organizations). In today's world the most critical issue is arguably how to achieve sustainability of the wealth creation process at the global scale. Sustainability is not just environmental, it is also social and economic; the three are related. Sustainability can be undermined by limited rationality, imperfect knowledge and information, different and potentially conflicting interests, embedded power structures, shortsightedness, time inconsistencies, and a lot more. All these apply to business firms, especially MNEs, but they also apply governments, regional blocks (e.g.,

EU) and international organizations (e.g., the IMF, World Bank, and WTO). There appears to be a pressing need to increase the specialist information available, to engender enlightened practices and policies, to align interests and to try to address problems of time inconsistencies, and other constraints, all with an eye to effect governance that favors sustainable global wealth creation. This is in everybody's interest.

Clearly a grand objective such as the above is rather pretentious to hope to achieve, and indeed even too romantic. We are not deluded, we simply feel that dialogue, mutual understanding, sharing of knowledge and learning, can help us improve things—not reach perfection (which is probably a Chimera), but build on strength, and improve weaknesses to get better. Certainly there are weaknesses to be improved. One of our global board members once asked the delegates to tell him what was, in their view, the difference between the "Mafia" and "Big Business." Following a short silence, he continued that "the Mafia is organized crime, Big Business is very organized crime!" You need intimacy for such views to be aired by top business people themselves. Important, however, was that this joke was made not long before the Enron and similar scandals. Such scandals confirmed there was more to that joke than one might wish. It also showed that sometimes Big Business can also make mistakes, that policymakers now come to realize this, and that sometimes it is even not so easy to tell who is who and what is what. Unfortunately, things get far more tangled when it is recognized that (apart from being definitely less organized) big governments and big international organizations can be more of a problem that the solution, see Stiglitz (2002). Analyzing and debating frankly these issues can be an eye-opener, and help at least appreciate the enormity of what needs to be done, but also the need to keep trying. In our own little way, at CIBAM we are.

I purposely left the issue of funding until last. There has been much debate in the past 20 years or so about the importance of being self-funded, and certainly CIBAM is based on this model. In practice this means that the various CIBAM events and activities (which also include a bi-annual newsletter entitled *Gloquacious,* an Annual Report and a Profiles Book) are funded by the members. These cannot be the academics (who can hardly survive on notoriously low academic salaries), so it had to be the business members. Of course, it could well have been the government too, and also the university and/or the school. These are vexed issues; with the government we did not try enough due to the usual time pressures (although we were twice sponsored by the DTI and BERR, thanks to the efforts and support of Vicky Pryce), while to the university and the school, we pay overheads. Clearly, one can understand universities which help create so much wealth, but only manage to capture a tiny fraction of it, yet every case is different. I feel CIBAM and "products" such as the Symposium are "public goods" with external spillovers which are often very hard to quantify. In such cases, we know from our public economics, that non-excludability, non-revelation of preferences and free-riding are likely to lead to under-provision. This may explain why there are not many CIBAMs and that CIBAM itself is now at a crossroads.

CIBAM at a Crossroads

Throughout its existence CIBAM relied on an annual donation by its board members, to fund its activities. No CIBAM member receives payment for these, the funding covers the administrative and research support, as well as the cost of the Symposia and the other activities. Over the years the activities have increased by a multiple of at least 10. Funding could not follow for a combination of reasons that include increasing overheads by the university and the school, little practical recognition of the work put into Symposia by the school (indeed changes in rules which recognize almost all other "administrative tasks" but the Symposia); increasing "professionalization" of the various functions in the school, such as human resources and finance, which increase the costs of communication and coordination and can contribute to making things sometimes unyielding; the need to cover expenses for some eminent speakers (we normally relied on people paying themselves for the "honor," which does not work with some professional speakers, who at the very least request, quite legitimately, their expenses) and others. All these led to a very small group of people (mainly the director) spending increasingly more time at no financial benefit and gradually at a large and increasing "opportunity cost," in terms of foregone income (e.g., from executive education) and time (e.g., for research). All these require substantial additional funding, which in turn require time and other resources as well as additional support from within and without the university and the school. There has been progress in this direction under the inspired leadership of the Judge by Arnoud De Meyer. De Meyer embraced the concept of Centers and the Symposia and contributed to their success in various ways (e.g., by waving overheads and organizing joint events, such as the present one). Such help gives us optimism and keeps us walking!

THE SYMPOSIUM ON "GREEN BUSINESS AND GREEN VALUES"

This section provides a summary of the Symposium's proceedings; it has been produced by Erik Lee, Zarko Maletin, Barclay Rogers, Igor Tumanov (MBA students 2008/2009, Judge Business School). The articles included in this volume elaborate on a selected number of the talks.

First Day—Thursday, 19 February 2009

Welcome Address

Dr. Christos Pitelis, CIBAM Director, welcomed the audience and noted that the Judge Business School (JBS) was celebrating its 20th year and recently ranked as the #3 business school in the United Kingdom by the *Financial Times*. He then introduced **Dr. Jochen Runde**, director of the

MBA Program at JBS, who highlighted how sustainability is part of the core of the MBA and how JBS will next year attempt to devote a specific track to sustainability. He mentioned individuals associated with JBS who have published items related to the environment and Judge's association with the Cambridge Center for Energy Studies, and its additional focus upon green issues in general.

Introduction

Dr Pitelis reviewed the history of CIBAM, which was established in 1995 and is a center within JBS. He mentioned how CIBAM explores the conditions for sustainable wealth creation in the global environment and achieves this by identifying the links between practice, theory and policy. CIBAM has been focusing on the Global Business Symposium and is proud of the global advisory board's foresight to discuss topics such as corporate governance and security, terrorism, and business before they became headline news. Due to time constraints, Dr. Pitelis highlighted that enlightened self-interest and national government regulation policies are necessary but not sufficient to create sustainability values. Then Dr. Pitelis introduced the main topics of the symposium and left the floor to **Dr. Noreena Hertz**, CIBAM associate director.

Opening Panel: "Green Business and Green Values: Issues"

The opening panel was chaired by Dr. Hertz who invited the panelists to introduce the crucial issues affecting green business and green values. She mentioned that in the wake of recession there is talk about shifting focus away from sustainability and human rights, but inferred that by the end of the Symposium, it would be made clearer than ever that this *is* the moment to address these issues.

"A Green Finance?"

Mr. James Twining (Associate Principal, McKinsey & Co.)

Mr. Twining focused his discussions around climate change and the economy: the myth versus realities. He mentioned the upcoming meeting in Copenhagen which will re-examine the Kyoto Protocol. Furthermore, he mentioned how detractors have claimed that in light of the recession, the focus should be on the economy, but Mr. Twining maintains that is the exact reason to look at sustainability because focusing on sustainability will help the economy.

Mr. Twining then discussed six myths and provided evidence to support his point of view which maintains that with market-based incentives, the world can enjoy increases to the economy through sustainable recovery.

Myth 1: We can wait.

Reality: We have a decade or less to act; waiting will significantly increase risks and costs. Research shows that there is an 80% chance of maintaining a less than 2 degrees Celsius rise in temperature if we can limit carbon to 400 ppm; however, if carbon is reduced to only 500 ppm the chance of maintaining a 2 degree Celsius temperature increase drops to 40%. The longer we wait, the more we will have to do, and a delayed reaction may render it impossible to keep carbon below 450 ppm.

Myth 2: We should fix the economy first.

Reality: Fixing the economy requires reducing fossil fuel dependence; otherwise, we will sow the seeds of the next crisis. People say the subprime crisis is the core issue, but as Thomas Friedman points out, borrowing money from China to buy oil from the Middle East and then burning it, doesn't make much sense. The United States currently has 2.4% of reserves, but uses 24% of the global oil. To avert a global oil crisis America must make structural changes toward this.

Myth 3: Reducing emissions will cost too much.

Reality: The "costs" of reducing emissions comprises investments that are manageable, and in many cases highly profitable. Mr. Twining presented a global greenhouse gas (GHG) abatement cost curve which examined 200 choices versus their abatement potentials. Low-carbon technologies have made great strides, and future learning curves will likewise be profitable. The carbon count can be kept at 450 ppm if £800 million per year are invested by 2020, £1.2 trillion by 2030.

Myth 4: Reducing emissions will reduce growth and cost jobs.

Reality: Clean energy investments will likely stimulate growth, create jobs, and spur carbon productivity. Incremental costs boost investment for GDP counts; the key is that incremental borrowing does not strain the economy or borrowing rates. He showed evidence that potentially 3.5 million jobs could be created in the United States by 2028.

Myth 5: Only developed countries need to (or should) act now; developing countries can wait.

Reality: We won't solve the problem unless developed and developing countries act together . . . now! A reduction of 17 Gt CO_2e is needed by 2020 and only a 5 Gt CO_2e reduction can be achieved in developed countries utilizing current technologies. Mr. Twining claims the abatement math does not add up and cannot be met without significant reductions from developing countries. It is necessary for developing countries to hit 90% of abatements for 450 ppm to be achievable.

Myth 6. Markets and regulations are in opposition.

Reality: Market and regulation can play complementary roles. Cap and trade, tax, and regulation are all methods and incentives that can be utilized to structure for success. There is no silver bullet; incentives will help, but government regulation is also required to hit targets.

In summary, Mr. Twining said that investments can stimulate growth in jobs, near term, and help create a long-term stable economy. The costs are manageable, but the key will be in achieving consensus among the192 nations in Copenhagen to work together on these very necessary and important issues.

"Doing Good Is Good Business"

Mr. David Roth (CEO, The Store, The WPP Group)

Mr. Roth's key message was that "doing good is good business" presented from a marketing and retailer's perspective. He noted that unlike a few years ago, sustainability, environment, and social responsibility were never far from the headlines and boardrooms. CSR is not philanthropy wherein you give away small fractions of profit, but rather, it is a mindset that helps businesses think in terms of how to give the business direction, accountability and clarity.

Mr. Roth said that sustainability business cases help improve corporate profitability and reduce environmental impact—a win-win for both companies and customers. Making these changes though is inherently complex because the supply chain is long and interconnected. He asked the question whether businesses should continue to purchase from suppliers that were not doing good? Is it better for a company to walk away or should they work with suppliers to improve their practices, which costs money and time? He suggests that businesses should apply the following imperative: if your products could tell their story from cradle to grave, from raw materials to finished products, would you be ashamed or proud?

Mr. Roth noted that many retailers utilize sustainability as a marketing ploy, but that it demands integrity. The rules are clear, that utilizing a thin veneer is worse than not doing it at all because if a veneer is scratched and exposed, brand damage in this area can be fatal. He also noted how customers are requiring transparency, for example being able to trace jewelry components down the supply chain. This new openness will be rewarded by customers.

Mr. Roth then discussed how the marketing community has a responsibility to be a driver in fostering societies where consumption is sustainable and excessive consumption is unfashionable. He said the marketer's message should shift to make durability a positive and disposability a negative. Under the current economic climate, sustainability budgets will come under pressure and will likely be scaled back. Customers will spend less, but expect retailers and suppliers to be ethical on their behalf. Mr. Roth closed his presentation by stating that businesses need to demonstrate leadership and put forth a model for sustainable development, and that partnership between business, government, and NGOs will be required for success.

"Islamic Banking and Sustainability"

Mr. Khalid Abdulla Janahi (CEO, Dar al-Maal al Islami Trust)

Mr Janahi's presentation focused on values and education. He started his discussion focusing on green values and said that we are where we are today because of a lack of overall values and because of greed. He contends that it is a myth that developing countries want developed countries to suffer and that we need to find our real values as human beings. All the blame that everyone tries to place on everyone else needs to stop and that internal review must take place. He asked why trillions of China's money is sitting in the United States and not being used to improve conditions locally. He said that the Middle East lacks good health services and schools and thinks that treasuries will be the next bubble.

Mr. Janahi then turned the discussion to Islamic banking's basic value—asset-backed business, which adds value to community. Islamic banks were not allowed to speculate or create hedge funds and could only conduct asset-backed business—which is why their bottom lines were not as impacted by the recent financial collapse. With over £1 trillion on the balance sheet, Islamic banking is projecting a15–20% growth per annum over the next five years.

Mr. Janahi claims that education is the key to supporting green values. Green business does not equal green values; he pointed out that companies can be doing green business because they are greedy and want to make money. Doing good and having green values, is on the education side. He maintains that business is the main player, governments will be involved, and NGOs will not play as strong of a role. While he understands the importance of the environment, he believes that the future cannot be successful without health, education, and then the environment.

"A Role for Government"

Ms Elizabeth Anastasi (Economic Adviser–Sustainable, BERR)
Mr. Paul Drabwell (BERR representative)

Ms Anastasi discussed the key low-carbon economy issues facing the UK government. One fundamental issue is defining "green business" as this has evolved over time from environmental issues, renewable energy, and waste treatment to today's issues of carbon management and social responsibility.

Britain has made a legally binding carbon reduction target of 80% (relative to 1990) by 2050. The whole economy must take account of carbon commitments and to an extent "green" their operations with the emphasis that all businesses and sectors understand the implications of these commitments.

Ms Anastasi relayed the current global size of the low-carbon economy, as standing at £3 trillion, with the UK sector accounting for £100 billion, employing 880,000 people, and a forecast growth rate greater than 4.5% annually to 2015. These values are slightly higher than normal because they include environmental goods and services, renewable energies, emerging low carbon, and waste treatment, so that it can illustrate how the entire economy is impacted.

Ms Anastasi then noted that the low-carbon economy is expected to grow strongly with increasing demand. She contends that the UK holds a comparative advantage in a number of areas that can develop green business opportunities, such as software, electronic machinery and equipment, and business and financial services; but she admits that barriers exist. Failures to take up "negative cost" solutions from an abatement cost analysis perspective suggests that limited availability of information, poorly aligned incentives, or problems with accessing necessary finance reflect barriers in the marketplace. She said the government's goal is to identify where issues exist and how to help resolve them, as well as push through the necessary changes.

Ms Anastasi said, looking forward, that the current economic climate has presented businesses across the board with considerable challenges and likely pushed climate change and other environmental concerns to the wayside, but that the longer-term challenges must not be lost. Short-term actions such as improved energy or resource efficiency can achieve both short- and long-term objectives, but the central issue is to ensure that business continues to increasingly take account of their environmental footprint in their day-to-day operations and investment decisions. Finally, a key issue for government is to help business make the transition to a more sustainable, low-carbon future by ensuring that the supporting infrastructure is in place—whether that is in terms of improving physical infrastructure, supporting innovation and R&D, or ensuring that the skills of the workforce are sufficient to meet these challenges.

Second Day—Friday, 20 February 2009

Opening Lecture

"Are Markets Enough?"

Sir Crispin Tickell (Director of the Policy Foresight Program at the James Martin 21st Century School, Oxford University)

Sir Crispin said that the answer to the question Are markets enough? was No. The current financial crisis had been partly caused by unregulated use of markets. It had served to obscure the still greater crisis over the growing human impact on the environment. All this would be taken up at Copenhagen in December later this year at the conference to replace the Kyoto Protocol. The central message was that we had to think differently across the spectrum, which included the place of market forces.

We had first to recognize that our current situation was unique. Other societies and civilizations had collapsed before for environmental and other reasons, but the circumstances of today had not happened before. As a title of a recent book put it: we had "Something New Under the Sun." The new circumstances included human proliferation, degradation of land, dependence on energy from diminishing stocks of fossil fuels, destruction of other species and damage to ecosystems, rise of sea level, pollution of both salt and fresh water and not least destabilization of climate worldwide. A new factor was the development of new technologies which, as the current president of the Royal Society had remarked, meant that our civilization had no more than a 50% chance of surviving this century.

Sir Crispin said that there was no such thing as a free market and never had been. All markets operated within rules, whether explicit or implicit, which together constituted a framework, which if it were any good should be in the public interest and for the public good. The way in which we measured current values in our consumer society was seriously askew. The shortcomings of "growth," GDP/GNP, and the like, were at last being recognized, notably in the *Financial Times* at the end of January this year. New systems of economic measurement, to include externalities and true costs, were now being examined by a group including Joseph Stiglitz and Amartya Sen. Sir Crispin hoped it would bring out the artificiality of much current economics including the current distinctions between developed, developing, under-developed and even over-developed countries. In many ways China and India came into all these categories.

Sir Crispin said that the change of mind necessary was already taking place, not least in the business community. Here he referred to the Stern review of November 2007 and Al Gore's film *An Inconvenient Truth*. He referred to the importance of education in developing green values. The best way to help people was to show them how to help themselves. Obviously, we needed to reduce carbon emissions and invest in new sources of energy. We had to think again about the design of cities and the future shape of business and industry. From his own contacts with business enterprises, top management was often less flexible than middle management with whom the future lay.

In concluding Sir Crispin said that there were three main factors of change, all of them flowing from proper appreciation of risk. We needed genuine leadership from above; pressure from universities, business, and the public generally from below; and, regrettably, benign catastrophes where cause could be safely attributed to effect. To the question What's in it for business? the answer was survival: how to assess risks and make the best use of opportunities.

Panel: "Challenges"

The panel was chaired by **Dr. David Reiner,** Director of the M.Phil. in Technology Policy Program at Judge Business School, who introduced the speakers of the panel.

"The Sustainability Challenge"

Prof. Charles Ainger (Visiting Professor in Engineering for Sustainable Development, University of Cambridge)

Prof. Ainger started the presentation with a discussion of the triple bottom line, which reflects a supposed balance between the environment, economy and society from a business perspective. He stated that in the current world he thinks too much emphasis is placed on the economy, causing a system imbalance. He said we act as if the benefits of the economy override everything else and that by following this path, damage is inevitable. For example, we try to use technology to address identified environmental issues.

Prof. Ainger finds the paradigm of the triple bottom line out of date and suggests that the correct structure would place society within the environment and the economy within the society. Society is an interface within the environment through resources and waste. The environment places limits on the society (through ecological and carbon footprints). Society is qualified through the quality of life for people and their communities (human development index, HDI). The economy creates jobs and wealth, and the fair distribution of these by serving the other two components.

Prof. Ainger elaborated on the UK government's Sustainable Development Strategy and presented data about the measurement of ecological footprints per person, by country, in 2005. Currently there is at average an impact of 2.7 global hectares per person, but the target is 1.44 hectares per person. He presented country data from 2006 for the HDI which measures the fulfillment of social and economic needs. Currently the global average is 0.747 with a target of 0.800, but there is a tremendous global imbalance.

He then reflected on Prime Minister Gordon Brown's statement on a "new deal for the world's poor," views of the J. Hansen Group about the urgency to target atmospheric CO_2 and John Schellnhuber's view about the need for a new "industrial revolution to start now." Prof. Ainger then proceeded to reflect on the opinion of Michael Porter, who believes that a healthy rate of innovation increases the likelihood that new technologies will solve the problems of the current trade-off between goals such as health, environment, safety and short-term economic growth.

At the end of his presentation, Prof. Ainger offered that business schools fail to address these issues and in general do not teach sustainable business. He reiterated the importance that businesses serve sustainable development, both locally and globally.

"The Energy Challenge—Convenience, Cost and Climate"

Mr. Edward Hyams (Chairman, Energy Saving Trust)

Mr. Hyams started his presentation with a discussion of the geometric rise in the use of energy-consuming equipment in business and in the home over the past several years. This increase goes hand in hand with improving lifestyles and well-being. He believes that society at large will be unwilling to forego the potential benefits associated with the rise in energy consumption even in the face of rising costs and climate worries.

Mr. Hyams illustrated this increase by presenting a graph on energy usage in previous decades, showing that the average household 20 years ago had 17 electric items, but by 2000 this had increased to 47. Energy is being used more efficiently, but more energy is needed, and it is estimated that by 2020, we will use more energy on entertainment than all of the energy that was used in 1970.

Mr. Hyams discussed how investments on the supply side are long term and that the right price signals are necessary to be mobilized. At the same time, governments are trying to force energy companies to bring the costs down, so how do we find the balance to make the proper new investments without the upside of profit?

Mr. Hyams discussed The New Electricity Trading Arrangements (NETA) and presented data from National Grid, showing that highly instable marginal energy prices do not support investments in the long run. He offered that no one is going to invest in low carbon because the price support is not there. He argued that the price will not go down as long as the politicians are involved in setting a cap.

Mr. Hyams discussed the UK target of 80% reduction by 2050, saying he thought it was technically possible; however, he thinks that we need to start now and use every tool available, including education. Mr. Hyams made a reference to two research documents on the rise in domestic equipment from the Energy Saving Trust: "The Rise of the Machines" and "the Ampere Strikes Back." These articles suggest that methods to improve the situation include better use of renewable energy sources (solar, nuclear, wind energy) and other approaches like proper investment of insulation in old and new buildings.

From the business side, Mr. Hyams argues that there is a better understanding of the situation from large businesses, less so from small and medium-sized businesses. In the end, he mentioned the need for an honest approach in making a change, and addressed the lack of political will, in the UK, in Europe and globally.

"The Challenge of Sustainable Games"

Mr. David Stubbs (Head of Sustainability, London Organizing Committee of the Olympic Games and Paralympic Games Ltd.)

Mr. Stubbs detailed how the London 2012 Olympic and Paralympic Games were planning to use the power of the Games to inspire change and embed sustainability in the long term for everyone by providing an example on the biggest stage.

Mr. Stubbs began with the idea that the key to sustainability is in how to bring changes to a level that ordinary people can understand and implement. He said that the Olympics are the world's largest event which could be used to promote sustainability with 2 million visitors, 10.5 thousand athletes, many journalists, and countless viewers across the world.

While elaborating on the role of the organization for the London Games, he provided examples of how they are striving to achieve sustainability. One of the first decisions was to choose Stratford as a place for over-all activity since it offered 500 acres of land and a location close to the city center. This area is among the poorest communities in London, but is very multicultural with 300 spoken languages, and its construction provided the opportunity to uplift the entire community area.

Mr. Stubbs elaborated on embedding sustainability in the day-to-day activities of the organization while educating workers, including 70,000 volunteers, on the sustainability goals. He further explained the process of providing sustainability with all of the activities organized, starting with travel, accommodation, entertainment, food, heating, lighting and clean-up. He said that opportunities existed to creatively solve sustainability issues in terms of seating, cabins, cabling, safety barriers, and temporary materials; and that the organization has engaged the best minds in the country to address these issues. Further he discussed their joint efforts with sponsors (Adidas, BP, BT and BA) in accomplishing sustainability through their corporate responsibility programs.

At the end Mr. Stubbs addressed the issue of determining how to monitor and measure the improvements that are being implemented, and how to ensure that sustainability is a core value in all that we can do.

Panel: "Solutions 1: Business"

The panel was chaired by **Mr. Peter Thoren,** executive vice president at Access Industries. Mr. Thoren briefly summarized the results of the previous discussions and touched upon safety, sustainability and green values as achieved by Access Industries and then introduced the panel speakers.

"Governance and Sustainability"

Mr. Jack Keenan (CEO, Grand Cru Consulting Ltd.)

Mr. Keenan began by taking a different look at "sustainability," namely, the role of the board of directors in ensuring the sustainability of profits in the company as the business reduces its impact on climate change. He asked whether we could add mechanisms to the Combined Code to ensure sustainable development of business. Mr. Keenan pointed out that the UK Combined Code is a terrific model which is well established and followed by many other countries, although it mostly contains principles rather than rules. Every company in the UK must announce that it complies with the code or explain why not. Mr. Keenan believes that within the code today we already have everything we need to ensure sustainability of a company, as managers must report the risk profile analysis to the board of directors twice a year. This risk profile analysis must contain the description of major risks threatening the company and the plan to mitigate those risks. It is important to note that, over the past year, of all of the major UK corporations none have claimed to have not complied with this risk analysis principle.

Mr. Keenan then proceeded to present a simple tool for risk assessment called the "Risk Matrix" which has been used at Diageo. It is a two-dimension matrix, with the horizontal axis being the probability of a risk a company might face, and the vertical axis being the costs of this risk, or a potential loss caused by risk occurrence. Since you report to the board twice a year, you can also show how the position of a particular risk has changed since last time. It has proved very useful to assign a person responsible for a certain risk in the matrix and its mitigation. Mr. Keenan then mentioned a few practical examples illustrating the use of the Risk Matrix, and also appropriate and inappropriate risk mitigations reported to boards.

According to Mr. Keenan, despite the fact that most companies in the UK reported to the boards the analysis of their major risks, quantification and mitigation of those risks, there have been a couple of cases in the past when companies failed to comply. As an example, the head of the risk assessment department for a large multinational bank had been fired by the CEO for identifying significant risks which the company faced at that time; moreover, he was replaced by a person who had no prior risk assessment experience. Furthermore, the auditors invited by the CEO said that the fired head of the risk assessment department had not been a team player. Mr. Keenan wrapped up his presentation by saying that despite the fact that risk assessment is a part of the Combined Code, sadly it has not been followed rigorously enough by chief executives.

"Demonstrating Goodness"

Mr. Michael Littlechild (Director, GoodCorporation)

Mr. Littlechild suggested distinguishing between a company which professes that it has green values, ethical behaviour and social responsibility and a company which really is oriented around these values. The question he raised was how we can understand whether a company is truly green-oriented and whether green orientation is part of its approach toward doing good business.

Mr. Littlechild then discussed the three broad approaches which companies utilize to demonstrate their goodness. The first approach is re-branding. As an example, BP—an oil company producing oil, gas, and petroleum; drilling for oil; using pipelines and the like—has come up with the green flower as a brand to show its new green approach. Second, companies started clubbing (i.e., joining groups of businesses and associations with similar high values for social responsibility). Business in the community, for example, created the "Companies that Count league table." The third approach is that companies produce Corporate Social Responsibility reports. These reports have become broader and may now cover various topics from the environment to philanthropy, but Mr Littlechild doesn't believe that these reports are of much use to the general public.

Mr. Littlechild provided an example of the web report of Barclays Bank where the CEO mentions the efforts put into achieving its CSR goals. This was followed by information from a BBC investigation which revealed that some of the bank's employees from the call centers demonstrated complete ruthlessness to the customers. Mr. Littlechild supported this "conflict of deeds and words" with other examples in which the realities of companies' attitudes to their clients were not as good as they were presented to the public.

According to Mr. Littlechild, this conflict shouldn't happen, as most companies invite independent auditors to ensure the reports, but when reading the fine print, the audits do not amount to substantial backing. Mr. Littlechild provided an example of British Nuclear Fuels plc. This report was checked and approved by Ernst & Young, with the disclaimer that the non–Environment, Health & Safety data had not been examined.

Mr. Littlechild then stressed that the production of a single report requires significant sums of money, including the auditors' fees. Reports, however, have many problems: data which is difficult to decipher, absolute numbers that are difficult to compare with others, limited self cross-examination, opacity, and limitations of assurance. Mr. Littlechild asks whether these are even worth doing.

Mr. Littlechild highlighted a few indexes that tell you how "good" the business of a company is: ISO 14001, BITC Corporate Responsibility Index, FTSE4Good, and the DowJones Sustainability Index. Mr. Littlechild showed that the FTSE4Good actually underperformed the FTSE-AllWorld index, and asked the audience members to arrive at their own conclusions.

Mr. Littlechild then introduced how GoodCorporation looks at the actual steps and actions a company actually performs, as opposed to things which it reports. Finally, he discussed what he thought companies should do to be sustainable. In his opinion, companies shouldn't publish any reports but keep them on their websites instead and update them regularly. These reports should reflect the real business practices, not just the trimmings, and he also thought that companies should look for independent verification of how they do business, not how good their reports look.

"Entering the New Era"

Dr. Noreena Hertz (Associate Director, CIBAM)

Dr. Hertz began by stating the importance of understanding the current danger to our environment, climate and sustainable development, and the fact that this threat has worsened with the current collective global financial crisis, which is distinctive from the Russian crisis, dot com crisis, and other such crises. She remarked that this is the end of the era of old-type

Gucci capitalism, which is the Anglo-American version of capitalism when the markets remained mostly unregulated and the governments preferred not to interfere in them. The Gucci capitalism era was the time when the power between the governments and businesses shifted toward businesses. It was the era of religious beliefs in market stability, equity, justice, and freedom, but in reality, it was the era when CEOs could earn up to a 1000 times the salary of their average worker, and hedge funds made billions of dollars. It was the period in which success was measured by the amount of money you had, and when it was a shame not to have a Gucci handbag.

Dr. Hertz says we are now entering the new era in which cooperation, collaboration and communication are at the core, the era which she called Coop capitalism. Dr. Hertz named five reasons why she thought we were entering this new era:

1. The public is angry, and this anger is caused not just by the bankers and their huge bonuses. Governments and businesses will have to declare clearly whether they would like to take the public side or not.
2. We are at the period of history when governments have an unprecedented mandate to intervene. A recent study in the United States showed that over the half of the population would now like the government to intervene directly in free markets. A few examples of industries to watch for changes in soon are the fast food sector and healthcare and pharmaceutical companies.
3. The downside of globalization is becoming apparent with the recent global economic downturn. The fact that Taiwan predicts a huge drop in the GDP in the coming year shows that we are now collectively responsible and linked to the economic downturn. We now see discussions about global regulatory mechanisms to deal with finance, but politicians should also have the similar bodies to deal with the environment and social issues.
4. It is no longer post-1945 settlement, and we are entering new geopolitical configurations. There is little reason to feel that Anglo-American values will remain dominant in the world. China, India and Brazil have never had Gucci capitalism; instead, they had their own models of development. These countries are going to have more of a voice on the international stage, and the rest of the world will likely listen to them in order to achieve collaboration.
5. Dr. Hertz doesn't believe it's just at the inter-governmental level where more cooperation is forthcoming; it is also at the individual level. She cites examples of individuals pulling together, similar to what was seen during the Great Depression, where individuals are giving goods away for free via the Internet instead of selling them.

Dr. Hertz ended by emphasizing the importance of the current moment and noted that the audience consisted of very influential people from business, government and academia. She implored that we make the effort to pull together and make our next generation safe, secure and happy.

Panel: "Solutions 2: Government, NGOs, Academia"

The panel was chaired by **Prof. J. C. Spender,** Visiting Professor, Center for Business Performance, Cranfield School of Management. Prof. Spender introduced the speakers for the panel.

"Green Values in Communities: Origins and Practice"

Dr. Michael Pollitt (Assistant Director of the ESRC Electricity Policy Research Group and Reader in Business Economics, Judge Business School)

Dr. Pollitt provided the ethical context for green values in communities. Dr. Pollitt addressed the ethics underlying the Stern Review and drew attention to the importance of—and debates surrounding—the Social Discount Rate. He explored the role of individual values as drivers of individual action. In the absence of value drivers and social norms, regulatory approaches are unlikely to work and may result in distributional problems with pricing (e.g., higher heating bills for the poor). He discussed the roots of value drivers and highlighted the critical role of religion in forming values. He explained that almost all major Christian denominations in the United States have expressed strong support for sustainable development and de-carbonization. According to Dr. Pollitt, the moral case for action on climate change is strong, and companies may play an important role in helping to weave the social fabric to support climate change initiatives.

"A Green New Deal?"

Ms Ann Pettifor (Executive Director, Advocacy International)

Ms Pettifor put forth the case for a Green New Deal. Inspired by Franklin D. Roosevelt's New Deal program, The Green New Deal Group propose a modernized version to tackle the current crash: the interlinked crises of climate change, recession, and energy depletion. Ms Pettifor emphasized the spreading usage of the Green New Deal concept and explained the need to build an alliance among industry, labor, and the green movement "to challenge the dominance of the finance sector over the real economy and the ecosystem."

Ms Pettifor set of the pillars of the Green New Deal as

- Policy autonomy for governments
- New checks, balances, and directions
- Low, low rates of interest—short and long, safe and risky
- Transforming our tax system

- Security for our pensions and savings
- Jobs, more jobs and secure jobs
- Warm homes in winter
- UK showing real-world leadership

Ms Pettifor argued for a fundamental re-formulation of our economy to address the current challenges.

"A Low-Carbon Industrial Strategy"

Prof. Vicky Pryce (Chief Economic Adviser and Director General of Economics, BERR)

Prof. Pryce addressed the transformation required to move to a low-carbon economy. Prof. Pryce explained that carbon constraints will require a shift in the way we work and live, and emphasized that "no sector and no business will be unaffected." She argued that the economic case for tackling climate change urgently is clear—quoting from the Stern Review that climate change is the "biggest market failure the world has seen."

Prof. Pryce suggested that the government's role was to set the framework for moving forward. She argued that markets are vital to addressing climate change but may not be sufficient. She highlighted several recent government initiatives, including the incorporation of green objectives into fiscal stimulus actions, measures to support business in the environmental and low-carbon areas, and support for the automotive industry based around low carbon. She stated that government must show leadership, and reinforced the importance of engaging with business in policymaking. According to Prof. Pryce, "we've all become passionate believers in saving the world." The only question is how to best do it.

Summing Up

Prof Spender underscored the need for a new way of thinking to meet these challenges. He explained that global destablization—climate change, biodiversity losses—suggests that the current system is broken. He stressed the need to develop priorities as "this is a way to avoid people selling their wares in new guises." He also noted that it is difficult to drive a wedge between image management and the global challenges. In Prof. Spender's view "CSR is another form of marketing."

Prof. Spender opined that humans can only know things in two ways:

- As observers (our understanding of nature)
- As inventors (our understanding of our own creations)

According to Prof. Spender, humans cannot understand ecology because "we didn't create it." We can, however, understand our own creations (e.g., economics). For this reason, he suggested that we focus on our own creations as a way to make progress.

CONCLUSION

Today greenness is goodness. Non-greenness is not an option. It is therefore critical to advance thinking on why and how business, consumers and policymakers can contribute to the goal of sustainable global wealth creation. The present volume aims to make a contribution in this direction.

REFERENCES

Cohen, R. B., Felton, N., Knoss, M., & Van Lier, J. (1979). *The multinational corporation: A radical approach.* Cambridge: Cambridge University Press.
Dunning, J. H., & Pitelis, C. N. (2008). Stephen Hymer's contribution to international business scholarship: An assessment and extension. *Journal of International Business Studies, 39*, 167–76.
Mahoney, J. T., McGahan, A. M., & Pitelis, C. N. (2009). The interdependence of public and private interests. *Organization Science, 20*, 1034–52.
Stiglitz, J. (2002), *Globalization and its discontents*, New York: W. W. Norton.

APPENDIX I

CIBAM Membership

Patron

Mr. Jack Keenan, CEO, Grand Cru Consulting Ltd.

Global Advisory Board

Sir Martin Sorrell, CEO, WPP, London (Chair)
Dr. Vassilis Apostolopoulos, CEO, G. Apostolopoulos Holdings SA
Mr. Len Blavatnik, President, Access Industries, Inc., New York
Mr. Michael Calvey, Managing Partner, Baring Vostok Capital Partners
Mr. Chun Chi Chou, Chairman, Sinyi Real Estate, Inc., Taipei
Mr. Jonathan Garner, Managing Director, Morgan Stanley
Mr. Tommy Helsby, Chairman—Eurasia, Kroll
Mr. Theodore Kyriakou, Group CEO and Vice Chairman, Antenna Group SA
Mr. Andrew Morgan, President—Europe, Diageo plc
Prof. Vicky Pryce, Senior managing Director, FTI Consulting
Mr. David Roth, CEO, EMEA and Asia, The Store—WPP
Mr. Andrew Smith, Chief Economist, KPMG Ltd.
Mr. Manfred Tuerks, Chairman, Sunwood International AG

Mr. Marc Verstringhe, Harry Hansen Fellow, CIBAM

Academic Advisory Board

Prof. Peter Buckley, Prof of International Business, Director of the Centre for International Business, Leeds University, UK

Prof. John Child, Chair of Commerce, Birmingham University; CIBAM Founding Director, UK

Prof. David Teece, Thomas W. Tusher Chair in Global Business, University of Berkeley, USA

Global Advisory Board Representatives

Mr. Jean-Michel Broun, Director, Baring Capital Partners (representing Mr Michael Calvey)

Mr. Eric Salama, CEO, The Kantar Group, WPP (representing Sir Martin Sorrell)

Mr. Peter Thoren, Executive Vice President, Access Industries (representing Mr Len Blavatnik)

Business Associates

Mr. Richard Broyd, Partner, Monitor Group, UK

Mr. Joseph Gold, CEO, Muza Gold Ltd, Israel

Mr. Marios Kyriacou, Senior Partner, KPMG, Greece

Mr. Patrice Muller, Partner / Director, London Economics, UK

Mr. Andrew Napier, Director, Prosequence Ltd., UK

Mr. Perran Penrose, Chairman, Penrose & Associates, UK

Mr. Kirill Slavin, Managing Partner, Slavin & Associates, UK

Mr. Minoru Tanaka, President, JMA Consultants Europe, Milan and CEO, JMA Consultants Europe, The Netherlands

Mr. Anthony Travis, Principal, Cabinet Gainsbury & Consorts, Switzerland

Mr. Antonis Vgontzas, Attorney-at-law, Greece

Mr. Peter Ward, Managing Director, Telos Partners, UK

Academic Associates

Prof. Tamir Agmon, Graduate School of Business, College of Management, Israel

Dr. Mie-Sophia Elisabeth Augier, Naval Postgraduate School and Stanford University, USA

Prof. Thomas Bernauer, Swiss Federal Institute of Technology, Switzerland

Prof. Michael Best, University of Massachusetts, USA

Prof. Patrizio Bianchi, University of Ferrara, Italy

Prof. Max Boisot, ESADE & INSEAD, Europe

Prof. Thomas Clarke, University of Technology, Sydney, Australia

Prof. Stewart Clegg, University of Technology, Sydney, Australia

Prof. Simon Collinson, Warwick Business School, UK

Prof. Giovanni Dosi, Sant'Anna School of Advanced Studies, Italy

Prof. Stuart Evans, Carnegie Mellon University, USA

Prof. Bruno Frey, University of Zurich, Switzerland

Dr. Simona Iammarino, University of Sussex, UK

Prof. Michael G. Jacobides, London Business School, UK

Prof. Neil Kay, University of Strathclyde, UK

Prof. James Love, Aston Business School, UK

Prof. Anita McGahan, Rotman School of Management, University of Toronto, Canada

Prof Paul McGuinness, Chinese University of Hong Kong

Prof. Lilach Nachum, City University New York, USA

Prof. Andy Neely, UK Advanced Institute of Management Research, UK

Prof. Mario Nuti, University of Rome, "La Sapienza", Italy and CNEM, London Business School, UK

Prof. Kenneth Oye, Massachusetts Institute of Technology, USA

Prof. Marina Papanastassiou, Copenhagen Business School, Denmark

Prof. Robert Pearce, Henley Business School, University of Reading, UK

Dr. Robert Pitkethly, University of Oxford, UK

Prof. Alan Rugman, University of Reading, UK

Prof. Hans Schenk, Utrecht School of Economics, The Netherlands

Prof. J. C. Spender, Cranfield School of Management, Leeds & Open University Business Schools, UK

Prof. Roger Sugden, University of Birmingham, UK

Prof. Haridimos Tsoukas, Athens Laboratory of Business Administration, Greece & University of Warwick, UK

Dr. Alain Verbeke, Haskayne School of Business, University of Calgary, Canada

Prof. Maurizio Zollo, Bocconi School of Management, Milan, Italy

Cambridge University

Dr. Shahzad Ansari

Prof. Jaideep Prabhu

Dr. Jane Collier

Dr. David Reiner

Dr. Gishan Dissanaike

Dr. Mark de Rond

Dr. Elizabeth Garnsey

Dr. Jochen Runde

Dr. Allègre Hadida

Prof. Ajit Singh

Dr. Charles Hampden-Turner

Dr. Philip Stiles

Ms Sally Heavens
Dr. Chander Velu
Dr. Chris Hope
Prof. Geoff Walsham
Prof. Martin Kilduff
Prof. Malcolm Warner
Prof. Stephen Littlechild
Prof. Peter Williamson
Dr. Michael Pollitt
Dr. Eden Yin

Director: Dr. Christos Pitelis
Associate Director: Prof. Noreena Hertz
External Liaison: Ms Marianna Vintiadis
Research Assistant: Ms Roumiana Theunissen

APPENDIX II

'Green Business and Green Values'
Program of Events
Thursday, 19 February 2009, Judge Business School

16:30–17.00	*Assemble with coffee*—Judge Common Room
17.00–17:05	*Welcome Address*—**Dr. Jochen Runde** (Director of the MBA Program, JBS) *on behalf of **Prof. Arnoud De Meyer** (Director of Judge Business School)*
17:05–17.20	*Introduction* × **Dr Christos Pitelis** (Director, CIBAM) Lecture Theatre III
17.20–19.05	*Opening Panel:* **"Green Business and Green Values: Issues"** *Chair:* **Dr. Noreena Hertz** (Associate Director, CIBAM) **Mr. David Roth** (CEO, The Store, The WPP Group)—*Doing Good Is Good Business* **Mr. James Twining** (Associate Principal, McKinsey & Co.)—*A Green Finance?* **Mr. Khalid Abdulla Janahi** (CEO, Dar al-Maal al Islami Trust)—*Islamic Banking & Sustainability* **Mr. Brian Titley** (Director of Performance and Evaluation, BERR)—*A Role for Government* Lecture Theatre III
19.05–19.15	*Transportation to Jesus College*
19:15–19:40	*Pre-dinner drinks*—Jesus College, Prioress's Room
19.40–21.30	*Gala Dinner*—Jesus College, Upper Hall
21.30–	*Informal drinks*—Doubletree by Hilton (Cambridge Garden House Hotel)

"GREEN BUSINESS AND GREEN VALUES"
Program of Events
Friday, 20 February 2009, Judge Business School

08:30–09.00   *Assemble with Coffee*—Judge Common Room

09:00–09.45   **Sir Crispin Tickell** (Director, the Policy Foresight Program, Oxford University)—*Are Markets Enough?*—Lecture Theatre II

09.45–11.15   *Panel:* **"Challenges"**—Lecture Theatre II
Chair: **Dr. David Reiner** (Director of the M.Phil. in Technology Policy Program, Judge Business School)
Prof. Charles Ainger (Visiting Professor in Engineering for Sustainable Development, University of Cambridge)—*The Sustainability Challenge*
Mr. Edward Hyams (Chairman of the Energy Saving Trust)—*The Energy Challenge—Convenience, Cost, and Climate*
Mr. David Stubbs (Head of Sustainability, London Organising Committee of the Olympic Games and Paralympic Games Ltd)—The Challenge of Sustainable Games

11.15–11.45   *Coffee break*—Judge Common Room

11.45–13.15   *Panel:* **"Solutions 1: Business"**—Lecture Theatre II
Chair: **Mr. Peter Thoren** (Executive Vice President, Access Industries)
Mr. Jack Keenan (CEO, Grand Cru Consulting Ltd.)—*Governance and Sustainability*
Mr. Michael Littlechild (Director of Good Corporation)—*Demonstrating Goodness*
Dr. Richard Broyd (Partner, Monitor Group)—*Environment and Business Strategy*

13.15–14.30   *Lunch*—Judge Common Room
Global Advisory Board Meeting—W4.04

13:30–14:30   **Board Members Only**

14.30–16.00   *Panel:* **"Solutions 2: Government, NGOs, Academia"**—Lecture Theatre II
Chair: **Prof. J. C. Spender** (Visiting Professor, Center for Business Performance, Cranfield School of Management)
Prof. Vicky Pryce (Chief Economic Adviser and Director General of Economics at BERR)—*A Low-Carbon Industrial Strategy*
Dr. Michael Pollitt (Assistant Director of the ESRC Electricity Policy Research Group, Judge Business School)—*Green Values in Communities: Origins and Practice*
Ms Ann Pettifor (Executive Director of Advocacy International)—*A Green New Deal?*

16.00–16.30   *Coffee break*—Judge Common Room

16.30–17.00   ***Summing up:*** **Professor Vicky Pryce** (Chief Economic Adviser and Director General of Economics at BERR)—Lecture Theatre II

2 Humans
Then, Now, and Looking Ahead
Sir Crispin Tickell

Humans are a remarkable animal species. Since the industrial revolution some 250 years ago, they have been acting in ways and multiplying at rates which affect the balance of life on the surface of the Earth as whole. The past is not necessarily a guide to the future. If there is any lesson to be learned from the past, it is that we have to think differently. The future is an unknown country.

Even the past was relatively unknown until very recently. We now have at last some idea of where we are coming from. Like all other living organisms we are joined in common descent and mutual dependency. Over time organisms tend to create and maintain the environment most favorable to them. Occasionally the system tips one way or another to the detriment of this or that among them. The biosphere is itself analogous to a living organism which corrects itself in response to hazards from within and without. As humans we are of course an infinitesimal part of the living world (0.00007% of estimated living species). Each of us has ten times more bacterial than body cells.

Our species is relatively new. No one was around to record the evolution of the first human-like creatures from ape-like ancestors in Africa some four million years ago. They left the trees for the savannah, became relatively hairless, and learned to walk upright on two legs, with consequences for the physiology of their growing brains. By at least half a million years ago, they had split into a variety of related strains. One of their offshoots may still have been living on the Indonesian island of Flores as recently as 12,000 years ago (a mere blink in geological time). Our own lot can first be identified between 200,000 and 150,000 years ago.

So that is where human history begins. Through analysis of fossils and work on current humans, we have been able to trace our genealogy back to so-called mitochondrial Eve (the female line) over 150,000 years ago, and Y chromosome Adam (the male line) between 90,000 and 60,000 years ago. It may seem amazing but all living humans may be descended from communities containing both, with of course millions of mixtures on the way. All other branches of humans, including our cousins the Neanderthalers, are now extinct.

It seems likely that there was some sort of crisis in human history which drastically reduced numbers and eliminated some of the lines of descent. Among the possibilities are abrupt climate change following the violent eruption of Mount Toba in Indonesia some 73,000 years ago, which initiated a severe cooling of the Earth within the Pleistocene ice ages. We know from recent history what big effects volcanic eruptions can have (Mount Laki in Iceland in 1783, Tambora in 1815 and Krakatoa in 1883), and Toba was a real monster among them. But there are other possibilities: some major epidemic like the Plague of Justinian in 540 AD, or the Black Death which devastated populations worldwide in the 14th century; or even a hit from space (if the object which devastated part of Siberia a hundred years ago on 30 June had hit London, there would have been nothing left within the M25 ring road).

The survivors of this major crisis, whatever and whenever it was, would have had many genes in common, and thereby influenced the character of subsequent generations. All modern humans are fairly close cousins. There are more genetic differences between Africans than there are between Africans and other humans, thereby indicating our African origins. Some recent work on the evolution of the bacterium *Helicobacter pylori* in our guts well illustrates this point.

A question which still arouses much controversy is when and why humans developed the attributes we all now take for granted: language, music, symbolic and interconnected thought, art in its many forms, including jewelry, advanced technical skills, and certain behavior patterns, including respect for the dead. Did this grow gradually out of development of tools for hunting, fishing and shelter, sexual competitiveness, the management of community relationships, or something else? Or was it the product of some genetic mutation which greatly advantaged some individuals and their descendants at the expense of others? Whenever the change took place, the extraordinary development of human brainpower, which has produced ourselves, occupies much less than 1% of all human history.

Over the last 40,000 years the human impact on the Earth has slowly and then rapidly increased. Hunter gatherers fitted easily, although sometimes uncomfortably, into the ecosystems of cold and warm periods of the Pleistocene. People migrated in response to changing conditions. But farming with land clearance between 10,000 and 8,000 years ago changed everything. It may even have changed the climate and, by affecting emissions of carbon dioxide and methane into the atmosphere, halted a return to colder conditions. With a vast increase in human population came towns and eventually cities. Tribal communities evolved into complex hierarchical societies.

Before the industrial revolution some 250 years ago, the effects of human activity were local, or at most regional, rather than global. Now the impact is indeed global.

The idea may be hard to accept, but in its long history with all its variations the Earth has never been in this situation before. In the words of the title of a recent book on environmental history, we confront "Something New Under the Sun." The problem is almost on a geological scale. No wonder the Nobel Prize winner Paul Crutzen with his colleague Eugene Stoermer should have named the current epoch the Anthropocene, in succession to the Holocene epoch of the last 10,000 years.

There are six main factors which have driven this transformation. Of these, population issues are often ignored as somehow embarrassing or mixed up with religion and the ideology of development; most people are broadly aware of land resource and waste problems, although far from accepting the remedies necessary; water issues, both fresh and salt, have had a lot of publicity, and already affect most people on this planet; climate change with all its implications for atmospheric chemistry is also broadly understood, apart from by those who do not want to understand it; how we generate energy while fossil fuel resources diminish and demand increases is another conundrum (now at last under serious discussion); but damage to the diversity of life on which our species critically depends has somehow escaped most public attention. Here we remain ignorant of our own ignorance. Yet in this area human destructiveness has been most evident over the last 10,000 years. Current rates of extinction could in the long run be the most important of all these factors for human welfare. All are interlinked, and all represent pressure on the natural environment.

There is now a seventh factor recent in human experience. They arise from the introduction of new technologies. Damage to the ozone layer, which protects ecosystems from harmful ultraviolet radiation from the Sun, was the first to receive major public attention. The eventual result was to establish international agreements to ban the manufacture and use of chlorofluorocarbons.

But this may only be the beginning. In a recent book by the President of the Royal Society, Sir Martin, now Lord, Rees explored the dangers arising from human inventiveness, folly, wickedness and sheer inadvertence. The ramifications of information technology, nanotechnology, nuclear experimentation and the rest have still to be understood and explored. His conclusion was to give our civilization only a 50% chance of survival beyond the end of this century. In broad terms we suffer from creeping impoverishment of the biosphere. As E. O. Wilson said in his book *The Creation*,

> We have, all by our bipedal, wobbly-headed selves, altered Earth's atmosphere and climate away from the norm. We have spread thousands of toxic chemicals world wide, appropriated 40% of the solar energy available for photosynthesis, converted almost all of the easily arable land, dammed most of the rivers, raised the planet sea level, and now, in a manner likely to get everyone's attention like nothing else before it, we are close to running out of fresh water. A collateral affect of all this

genetic activity is the continuing extinction of wild ecosystems, along with the species that compose them. This also happens to be the only human impact that is irreversible.

There has been some talk, notably among the religiously inclined, about a human obligation of "stewardship" of the Earth. If so the Earth had to wait a long time for the arrival of the stewards. Certainly the trilobites managed for over 250 million years without them. Looking at the human record of predation, exploitation and extinction of other forms of life since the current version of humans appeared over 150,000 years ago, I am reminded of James Lovelock's remark that "humans are about as qualified as stewards of the Earth as goats are gardeners."

But unlike goats, humans can change their minds if they develop the will to do so. Are we capable of establishing a lasting relationship of mutual benefit to the living Earth and those of its unruly inhabitants who are ourselves? How are we to recognize that the last 200 years or so have been a bonanza of inventiveness, exploitation and consumption which may not continue? All successful species, whether bivalves, beetles, bears or humans, multiply until they come up against the environmental stops, reach some accommodation with the rest of the environment and willy-nilly restore some balance. Are we near to those stops? Or do we think we are different?

Of course we think we are different; and because we are different, there is a lot we can do about the huge range of problems facing us. In fact most of the solutions are well known. Briefly we have to re-think some of the underlying assumptions on which we run our society. That means confronting the major issue of our own proliferation in all its aspects; looking again at a lot of economics; replacing consumerism as a goal; giving high priority to conservation of the natural world; working out new ways of generating energy; dispersing and to some extent localizing the ways by which we feed ourselves; managing and adapting to climate change, or as I prefer to call it climate destabilization; and creating the necessary institutional means of coping with global problems. In the future global village, we cannot afford to have too many village idiots.

We all suffer from the disease of what has been called conceptual sclerosis. Little is more difficult than learning to think differently, above all when problems go to the roots of the conventional wisdom. Old ideas haunt us like ghosts.

For me an immediate priority, spurred on by the current economic crisis, is to think differently about economics. Some, fortunately not all of us, tend to believe that greater material prosperity is an overwhelming priority, that resources can be exploited indefinitely, and that growth on the usual definition is good in itself: in other words ever upwards and onwards with free markets, free trade and continuously rising consumption. This is the philosophy of many economists and most politicians, at least until recently. The problem is exacerbated by some ingrained beliefs: that technology can always find an answer; that "development" or industrialization will raise living standards world wide; and that globalization will come to represent a benign mutation in human civilization.

Now at least many are looking again at how to measure human wealth and welfare. The key factor is costs. As has been well said, markets are marvellous at fixing prices but incapable of recognizing costs. Most costs—or externalities—are long as well as short term. All markets operate within rules, whether explicit or implicit, which together constitute a framework which, if it is any good, should be in the public interest. Who decides what is in the public interest? Most of the answer lies with governments, however chosen, who have the particular responsibility of listening to and guiding public opinion. This brings me back to the environment and the rest of the living world. However we look at it, the economy—the human economy—is a wholly owned subsidiary of the environment.

I turn to the future of our species in a world which is changing under human pressure before our eyes. Bear in mind that nearly all forecasting turns out to be wrong. We do well to expect the unexpected.

In his book *The Meaning of the 21st Century*, James Martin laid out what he saw as the prospects.

> The 21st century is like a deep river canyon with a narrow bottle neck at its centre. Think of humanity as river rafters heading down stream. As we head into the canyon, we'll have to cope with a rate of change that becomes much more intense—a white water raft trip down an unknown river with the currents becoming much faster and rougher—a time when technology will accelerate at a phenomenal rate.

He went on to identify the main challenges facing us. Some relate to the Earth as a whole: for example the natural disruptions known throughout history, volcanic explosions, earthquakes, impacts of extraterrestrial objects, changing climates, and variations in ecosystems, including patterns of disease, affecting all living creatures, from mushrooms to plants and such animals as ourselves.

In the short term all this will affect human migration between countries and continents, widening divisions between rich and poor within and between countries, increasing the already high vulnerability of cities, promoting the growth of terrorism, increasing the risks of war with unimaginably horrible weapons, and exhausting often irreplaceable resources. On this reckoning we will be lucky to come out the other side of the deep river canyon with anything like civilization as we know it.

But this is not the whole story. I want now to jump ahead a hundred years and, from this vantage, look backwards. In doing so, I shall assume (I hope correctly), that humans will have faced up to and coped with at least some of these problems. People are not stupid. So what will the world look like?

First they are likely to be living in a more globalized world. It should then be clearer whether the mutation was benign or not. There will certainly be a redistribution of political power away from the Unites States and Europe, and toward such former leaders in science and authority as China, India, and the Islamic world. This will be facilitated by rapid communication of all kinds. Ideas, units of information—or memes—will pass almost instantaneously between countries, communities and individuals. The wiring of the planet with fiber optics, cellular wireless, satellites and digital television is already transforming human relationships. For the first time there will be something like a single human civilization. More than ever humans can be regarded like certain species of ants, as a super-organism.

Human numbers in cities or elsewhere will almost certainly be reduced, but some people will live much longer, bringing its own train of problems. Their distribution will be different. It has been suggested that an optimum population for the Earth in terms of its resources would be nearer to 2.5 billion rather than—as now—more than 6.5 billion, or even 9 billion later this century.

Communities are likely to be more dispersed without the daily tides of people flowing in and out of cities for work. Agriculture will be more local and specialized with more reliance on hydroponics. Energy and transport systems will be decentralized. Archaeologists of the future may even wonder what all those roads were for.

Then there are other developments in information technology. They raise the question of evolution itself. At present we can alter isolated genes while disregarding the totality of what genes can do. James Martin has distinguished what he has described as primary, secondary and tertiary evolution. He suggests that:

> Primary evolution is the mutation and natural selection of species—a glacially slow process . . .
> Secondary evolution refers to the intelligent species learning how to create its own form of evolution. It invents an artificial world of machines, chemical plants, software, computer networks, transport, and manufacturing processes and so on. It learns how to manipulate DNA . . .
> Tertiary evolution refers to something which is just beginning on Earth. An intelligent species learns to automate evolution itself.

The idea of automated evolution needs some explanation. In a phrase it represents a vast acceleration of change. James Martin writes that with the machines we envisage today, it could be a billion times faster.

> Furthermore it will be incomparably more efficient. Darwinian evolution is described as being random, purposeless, dumb and Godless. Automated evolution is targeted, purposeful, intelligent, and has humans

directing it and changing its fitness functions on the basis of results. In Darwinian evolution, the algorithm stays the same. In automated evolution researches will be constantly looking for better techniques and better theory. The techniques of evolvability will themselves evolve.

Other applications of information technology range far beyond enumeration. Already chips have been inserted into humans for a variety of purposes. We can even insert extra chromosomes in the knowledge that they would not be heritable.

On the one hand humans may thereby be liberated from many current drudgeries. Soon houses may be able to clean themselves, robots may produce meals on demand, cars may drive under remote instruction, and evolution of desirable characteristics could even be automated. All this seems unimaginable when so many still have to trudge miles to collect fuel wood and water.

On the other hand humans could well become dangerously vulnerable to technological breakdown, and thereby lose an essential measure of self-sufficiency. Already dependence on computers to run our complex systems, and reliance on electronic information transfer, are having alarming effects. Here industrial countries are far more vulnerable than others. Just look at the effects of single and temporary power cuts. More than ever individuals feel out of control of even the most elementary aspects of their lives.

There is also a more sinister possibility. Some might wish to develop a subspecies of super-humans with genes tailored to specific requirements. In his fantasy *The Time Machine* of 1898, H. G. Wells foresaw a genetic division of humans into Eloi (or upper worlders) and Morelocks (or lower worlders). The Eloi lived in a happy sunlit world while the Morelocks lived mostly in caves, and did all the menial work for them: in short an exaggerated version of the slave world of the South in the United States before the Civil War.

How will the world be governed a hundred years from now? It would be romantic to think that democracy in one form or another will prevail worldwide. In practical terms we can say that good regulation will be more important than ever, particularly in nanotechnology. In the words of a recent book, we have to recognize that most things fail, whether they be organisms or human institutions. Already there is a movement of power away from the nation-state: upwards to global institutions and corporations to deal with global issues; downwards to communities of human dimension; and sideways by electronic means between citizens everywhere. It is hard to believe that nation states will exist in their present form. Already sovereignty of the kind enjoyed in the past has become an illusion. For global institutions I have long urged the creation of a World Environment Organization to bring together the present diverse and overlapping series of limited environmental agreements, and to be the partner of the World Trade Organization and other United Nations bodies and agencies. It might become the most important among them.

Let us hope without total confidence that by 2100 humans will have worked out and will practice an ethical system in which the natural world has value not only for human welfare but also for and in itself. The human super-organism must take its place alongside other super-organisms.For the long term I hesitate to speculate. We all have our own Leviathan. As Peter Ward once wrote: "The future stretches before us not as one long dark tunnel but as a series of vignettes of variable clarity, like a long avenue punctuated by street lights of differing luminosity." Tectonic plate movement will shift the relationship between land and sea. Changes in oxygen levels in the atmosphere may affect the viability of life itself. The human species may even change its shape, assuming some are still alive to tell the tale. For example, given the evolutionary significance of our brains and the current hazards of childbirth, we might imagine a sort of human marsupial in which women gave birth earlier in the reproductive process, and developed a kind of pouch.

As Thomas Hobbes said, as he approached death: "I am about to take my last voyage, a great leap in the dark." That is true for all of us; however, we measure and look forward to the future.

I sometimes wonder how long would it take for the Earth to recover from the human impact. How soon would our cities fall apart, the soils regenerate, the animals and plants we have favoured find a more normal place in the natural environment, the waters and seas become clearer, the chemistry of the air return to what it was before we polluted it? Life itself, from the bottom of the seas, to the top of the atmosphere, is so robust that the human experience could become no more than a short and certainly peculiar episode in the history of life on Earth.

Above all let us remember how small and vulnerable we are as creatures of a particular environment at a particular moment in time. We are like microbes on the surface of an apple, on an insignificant tree, in an insignificant orchard, among billions of other insignificant orchards stretching over horizons beyond our sight or even our imagining.

3 The End of Gucci Capitalism

Noreena Hertz

THE NEW DAWN

There are some who say that this current global financial recession, this recession stroke depression that is being felt in London and New York, in Madrid and Athens, will not impact upon the nature of capitalism. They say that we have been here before—faced and navigated our way through economic downturns—and that capitalism emerged unscathed. And they go on to say that five years from now capitalism will basically look as it did before the economic crisis began.

I understand this caution about predicting anything new, a reluctance to call the past era of capitalism's demise, but I do not agree with it. I believe the conditions *are* in place for a markedly different economic model to emerge from the carnage currently being wrought.

For I do not believe that what we are seeing today is just a variant of the Russian crisis, the dot com crisis, the Japanese crisis, or other crises that happened and had consequences but did not impact upon ideology or the fundamental trajectory of political and economic policy. I do believe that this first full crisis of globalization, this first collective lose-lose, this first blue- and white- and multicolored-collar recession is *so* profound, is already negatively affecting so many people all over the world, and is beginning to be generally admitted to being linked to the flawed ideological doctrine of the past 30 years, that it has a good chance of catalyzing a radical change of capitalism, catalyzing a radical change in the relationships between government, business, and society. These changes will have massive implications for nations, supranational institutions, corporations and individuals.

GUCCI CAPITALISM

I have named the past era of capitalism, Gucci capitalism. Gucci capitalism was an ideology born in the mid-1980s, the love child of Ronald Reagan and Margaret Thatcher with Milton Friedman its fairy godfather and Bernard Madoff its poster boy. It was an era whose fundamental assumptions were that markets should be left to self-regulate, governments should practice laissez-faire, and human beings are nothing more than rational utility maximizers.

In the era of Gucci capitalism shareholders were king, or rather those with significant enough holdings to have some clout. Society, employees, customers and those impacted by businesses' decisions were decidedly relegated to second place.

It was a period that promoted an almost religious belief in the market's ability to be not only a distributive mechanism but a deliverer of equity, justice and even freedom, despite the mounting evidence that in reality that wasn't actually happening and that in the very countries that adopted Gucci Capitalism most wholeheartedly, a gaping chasm was emerging between the economy and social justice. Under Gucci capitalism, British bankers took home salaries as much as 100 times that of an ordinary worker. In the United States hedge fund managers could earn over a billion dollars. Social mobility in both countries did not improve in 30 years.

It was a period in which Gordon Gekko's "Greed is good" mantra from the late 1980s movie *Wall Street* remained the motto for the next two decades. Risk was promoted by politicians and lauded by society, but responsibility was not accordingly aligned. It was an era in which success increasingly became something that was only measurable with money, and in which money became, in the financial sector especially, increasingly detached from physical assets or realizable potential. In the era of Gucci capitalism, it became more shameful not to have the latest pair of Nike sneakers or Gucci handbag than to be in debt. In the United States the average number of credit cards per person was nine.

It is no wonder that in an era with this its underlying ethos, regulators were too weak, bankers were too powerful, and checks and balances were not in place. In this era, the narrative that to be successful one had to have a bigger house and the newest line of the most fashionable brand was actively fed by bankers, mortgage brokers, credit card companies, and advertisers alike. With this the driving force in society, it wasn't a matter of *if*, it was a matter of *when*, the whole pack of cards would come tumbling down.

Once it did fall, the hollowness of its firmaments, its lack of foundations, was revealed for us all to see. Gucci capitalism was as lacking in real values, as focused on meaningless consumption, as short-termist and as superficial as its name suggests.

THE END OF A PARADIGM

But attacks and bouts of self-awareness can be short-lived, and paradigms are notoriously hard to shift. Are the conditions in place for a new form of capitalism, a form that I have named coop capitalism with values of co-operation, collaboration, coordination, community and communication at its heart, to emerge in its stead? I believe they are.

There are three key reasons why I believe this is so.

1. The Old Ideology has been Intellectually Discredited

Under Gucci capitalism human beings became caricatured, super-rational, selfish, profit and consumption maximizers. All the complexities of this big messy world were attempted to be reduced into mathematical models, charts, and matrices that could fit onto PowerPoint slides. And when the facts didn't fit the model, the matrix or the chart, they were not changed; instead, they were brushed under the carpet.

This of course had consequences that we now are all too aware of. There is now a recognition and a public admission that economists' forecasts and models were relied on far too heavily. And finally within economics and within the social sciences in general a well due debate has begun on the limits of the discipline and the beginnings of disentangling what were "truths" and what were in fact ideologies rather than facts.

This disentangling will continue to gain momentum. Economists such as myself and Paul Krugman, Joseph Stiglitz and Jeffrey Sachs, who had come to be considered "alternative" over the past decade, are now those being sought out to steer the recovery. Perhaps because we always realized the limitations of economics, and the importance of a more holistic approach. I, for one, have always incorporated sociology, history, behavioural science, psychology and even anthropology in my analyses. And this isn't revolutionary or radical, the greatest economists of the past whatever their political persuasion whether Schumpeter or Galbraith or Keynes or Hayek all understood that economics could not be put in a silo, and that to understand the world would take more than a few mathematical models. Adam Smith in addition to writing *The Wealth of Nations* wrote *The Theory of Moral Sentiment* recognized that the market was amoral—and that morality needed to be imposed upon it.

2. Governments now have a Mandate to Intervene

The second reason why a new model of economics looks likely to emerge is because a new mandate for government to intervene is now present; it simply was absent over the past three decades. In a recent survey conducted in the United States, the most traditionally hostile environment to government intervention, more than half of those surveyed now say that the free market should not be allowed to function independently. This is a seismic shift.

Banks are the first to see the impact of this with interventions being enshrined in law in the United States, the United Kingdom, and elsewhere. Although I don't predict such wholesale micromanagement by government of the private sector as a whole—nor would I condone it—I would warn any company that could be perceived to be acting against the public good that it now risks standing in the line of fire. Obvious industries to be targeted first are the fast food industry and big pharma. With health costs soaring, and governments needing to rein in expenditure, I predict more pressure on fast food companies to take responsibility for the obesity crisis and on pharmaceutical companies to deliver affordable medicines.

Under Gucci capitalism, mandating corporations to do things for a greater public good was rare. Now, especially given the braying public and media and a cycle of domestic elections looming, it will become increasingly the norm.

3. Other Countries with other Mindsets are in the Ascendency

The third reason for why we are heading toward a new era of capitalism is because a new configuration of geopolitical forces is emerging as a result of the rise of China, Brazil and India and the emergence of the G20. A new credible and cohesive body that is powerful, demands to be heard, and has limited if any allegiance at all to Gucci capitalism.

But it's not just that this new power bloc is likely to directly challenge the intellectual hegemony of Gucci capitalism. Combine this with a new U.S. administration, which already pre crisis talked about spreading the wealth and is committed to a multilateral ideal, and the fact that Continental Europe having been hit particularly hard by the global recession has a strong incentive to distance itself from an ideology that it did not spawn and never sat that well with its inherent communitarian values, and we have all the ingredients in place for a significant ideological shift.

THE RISE OF COOP CAPITALISM

Okay, so we are in the midst of an ideological shift. But am I right in predicting that it will take the form of coop capitalism?

Of course it is impossible to crystal ball gaze with absolute certainty. But by combining an analysis of the reasons for the demise of Gucci capitalism, with appropriate historical reference points, and on-the-ground observations with conversations with global movers and shakers and also polling data from the general public, I think coop capitalism describes the contours at least of what is likely to emerge from the ashes of the past.

Already we see evidence of new defining characteristics. We see a recognition at last that an interconnected world needs interconnected solutions, which of course doesn't mean that every country is going to adopt the same policy, nor that horse-trading will not take place (it already is), but that there will be moves toward common solutions and shared goals.

Discussions persist with regard to the creation of a global financial regulatory system, for example, despite the efforts of industry lobbyists to stymie its formation. But this is just the beginning. As we begin to see other crises through the same lens as the financial crisis (i.e., a collective and shared problem), it is likely that more global agreements, institutions and arrangements will be set up to address the myriad of *problems* that are generated by businesses and the collective actions of individuals, whose consequences spill over to the general public at large both domestically and overseas.

But it is not just at an intergovernmental level that we see the signs of more cooperation. The assumption of Gucci capitalism that we, as individuals were selfish, super-individualistic beings who only cared about maximizing our wealth, salaries, and resources, is proving to be more an expediency and a failing of mainstream economists than an accurate depiction of mankind.

While it is true that over the past two decades there has been a perceptible pressure to keep up with the Joneses, and a growing obsession with material worth, this may be more a case of nurture than nature. Anthropological studies show that societies that have less, share more, and recent work in behavioural economics has confirmed that benevolence is not alien to human nature. So whilst it may have been true that under Gucci capitalism there was a tendency to bowl alone, it might just not be the case that we are essentially individualistic.

More likely is that we are entering an age of pulling together, as was the case during the Great Depression and the Blitz, and that this will be one of this era's key defining characteristics. Its early days to show mass manifestation of this, but there are a few things we can point to the meteoric rise of the global "free cycle" movement whose members give stuff away for free rather than sell their goods on eBay; the rise in Japan of the notion of job sharing—where rather than having swathes of employees sacked, employees are choosing to work fewer hours so as to soften the collective blow, a principle now being copied in parts of Europe; or the fact that over a million baby caps were knitted by Brits for babies in developing countries, not *before* but *since* the financial crisis began.

Interestingly some non-traditional business models seem to fit within the coop capitalism rubric and are faring particularly well. One such business model is the women-run financial services company to which many Icelandic depositors ran after their macho bankers pushed their country over the edge. The brand "Innocent," the smoothie juice maker, is another example. This company is so committed to the environment that it pioneered making plastic bottles completely recyclable and positioned itself from the start as a company with values of social and environmental justice at its heart. And it sold a 20% stake in its company to Coca Cola, right in the midst of the financial crisis.

Of the non-traditional models, the cooperative movement offers a wealth of support for a cooperative model. From the cooperatives in Emilia Romagna in Italy, a region that is one of the most successful economically in Europe and the home of over 8000 cooperatives, to the Desjardin's Group, the financial cooperative in Quebec, that region's leading employer, to Switzerland where cooperatives are the largest private employer, this alternative model of organization has already made a huge impact on employment and economic success.

And importantly in a time of crisis cooperatives seem to be able to endure and survive longer than other companies. A recent Canadian government study concluded that cooperative businesses tend to last approximately two times longer than other businesses in the private sector. The stability of the cooperative enterprise, indicated by a low number of bankruptcies and the longevity of cooperatives, can be attributed in part to the fact that they are locally rooted in their communities. A quality that in the coming months of recession will in all likelihood help them endure better than other less-rooted competitors.

Indeed whilst the financial and ensuing economic crisis has had a negative impact on the majority of enterprises, cooperative enterprises around the world are showing resilience to the crisis. Financial cooperatives remain financially sound; consumer cooperatives are reporting increased turnover; worker cooperatives are seeing growth as people choose the cooperative form of enterprise to respond to new economic realities.

And then of course there's the rise and increased success of collaborative cooperative sharing models on the Internet which should not be seen as something apart from other sectors, but perhaps as a window into what might now work elsewhere. iPhone and Facebook have encouraged programmers to create applications for them, social networking sites are on the rise, and the open source movement with its poster boy stories—Linux and Apache—have been successful. The "open movement" in general encompasses "open design" where, in Helsinki, for example, there has been a revolution in the way old people's homes are being designed with the elderly being part of the design process, and open creation such as Wikipedia.

All these cooperative sharing models point to a multiplayer version of capitalism which encourages *all* parties to work together in pursuit of a common good.

Coop capitalism is the political-economic version of "Yes we can." With the emphasis on the "we," coop capitalism is a system with the potential to be more inclusive, more equitable and more participatory than what guided the world in the past. This system tends to fair rules, social justice and sustainability and reconnects the economy with what is right and just and meaningful. It is a system that allows everyone the potential to collaborate in common cause and doesn't leave society or its institutions to be shaped and fashioned only by those that shop at Gucci.

4 The Energy Challenge

Edward Hyams

UK emissions have to come down by at least 80% by the middle of the century if we are to meet our targets and play our part in counteracting man-made climate change. This is a big number, and it implies significant changes—but it does not have to mean that we sacrifice the way of life we are used to.

We have been used to having energy on tap—and to it being cheap. This state of affairs is not going to last. Energy is going to get more expensive, and what's more, the UK will have to import more fuel as its supplies of North Sea oil and gas run out. So fuel prices—for cars, for heating and cooking and for running our homes—are going to go up at the same time that we need to decarbonize our energy system. This gives us a double incentive to become "greener."

Becoming greener should not just be seen as being about making sacrifices—the huge changes that are needed will create massive opportunities for businesses throughout the supply chain and for customers to save money. In these recessionary times, there is also the opportunity to create large numbers of jobs in making and installing energy-efficient products to provide a boost to the economy at the same time as decarbonizing it.

There is enormous scope, for example, to make our homes more energy-efficient and we do not need to wait for some futuristic technology to be developed. We could save 20% of emissions by installing readily available technologies like loft and cavity wall insulation and gas-condensing boilers.

Many homes have solid walls so cavity insulation is not an option. Properly insulating these homes produces even more savings, but it is more expensive so we need to find ways of bringing costs down through economies of scale and innovative funding schemes.

Of course, there will be improvements in future, making measures such as floor insulation, improved glazing and LED lighting easily and cheaply available. We need to encourage the development and deployment of these technologies. The government has already taken some significant steps in this direction, mandating that by 2016 all new homes must be zero-carbon. It is not just the individual house that must be zero-carbon; developments must take into account low-carbon transport and renewable energy supplies.

All current houses must now have an Energy Performance Certificate when they are sold so buyers know the costs of buying a poorly insulated home. This measure would be more effective if introducing energy saving measures led to a reduction in council tax.

Another area that needs to be tackled is the private rented sector—landlords have no incentive to make their properties energy-efficient because it is their tenants, not they, who reap the benefits.

SMALL IS BEAUTIFUL—THE RISE OF MICROGENERATION

The government has said that by 2020, every home must be equipped with a smart meter. Smart meters are the building blocks of a smart grid, and they herald a revolution in the way energy is produced, the way the grid is managed and in the relationship between customer and supplier.

Smart meters mean that real-time communication between homes and the energy companies is possible. Why does this matter? It opens up the energy system in much the same way that the Internet did for the telecoms sector. Suppliers get a much better picture of demand, allowing them to manage the grid and their generating assets much more effectively. It also allows them to offer customers incentives to move their demand away from peak times, smoothing the demand profile and making existing capacity much more efficient.

But more importantly for customers, the smart grid will encourage them to generate their own energy and sell it back to the energy companies. Combined with the government incentive schemes for clean energy and renewable heat—to be introduced in 2010 and 2011, respectively—homes will be paid to generate energy using solar panels, ground- and air-source heat pumps, biomass and micro-CHP (combined heat and power) boilers, along with a range of other technologies.

The cost of many technologies, such as solar photovoltaics (PVs), is coming down significantly and over time we will probably see PVs routinely integrated into building materials such as roof tiles. Ground and air-source heat pumps will play a bigger role in heating, as will biomass, which has probably been under-emphasized by the government.

Eventually, fuel cells will finally become a viable option to power cars and homes. We may see renewable installations such as wind farms being used to produce hydrogen at off-peak times when prices are low. However, it is unlikely that large-scale energy storage will play a large role in the energy system in future. Instead, microgeneration will be widespread enough for us not to need storage.

As homes create their own power, large-scale generation will be undergoing its own revolution at the same time. The smart grid will be far better equipped to accommodate rising levels of renewable energy from wind farms on and off shore, from wave and tidal power and from smaller-scale power stations generating energy from the waste that we throw away. District heating schemes will see more electricity generated at a local level, with the heat created being piped into homes, schools, hospitals and businesses.

THE RISE OF THE MACHINES

We have seen a revolution in consumer electronics over the last three decades—we have gone from households with one TV in the living room to multimedia households with TVs in every bedroom, along with iPods, mobile phones, digital cameras and computers scattered about the home. In the kitchen, the stove has been joined by microwaves, juicers, bread makers and coffee machines. The washing machine now has a tumble dryer and a dishwasher for company and the fridge/freezer has bulked up and makes ice cubes. Many of these appliances have digital clocks so people feel they have to be kept on all the time.

Individually, all of these appliances have become much more energy efficient over the years, but because they have become more affordable, they have proliferated, and the net result is that energy use in the typical UK home doubled between 1972 and 2002. By 2010, it will have risen a further 12% from 2002, to exceed 100 TWh.

The current design of many of these gadgets does not help: the advent of remote controls means that some appliances no longer have off-switches, only standby. Standby means that you are using power, and spending money, even when you are not there—which will become increasingly unacceptable in an age of high energy prices and low carbon that will drive a push for energy efficiency.

Meanwhile, a whole new set of mobile devices has arisen because advances in battery technology mean that they can be charged at home and then travel with you. Mobile phones, MP3 players and digital cameras cut the need for disposable batteries, but few people realize that leaving their chargers switched on so they can plug in when they get home uses electricity even when they are not charging. Individually, the energy consumed is small, but if all homes in the UK (and every home has at least one mobile phone) left their chargers on, they would use enough energy to power 66,000 homes a year.

I can illustrate the extent of the changes from my own professional experience. I used to run an electricity transmission business, and 20 years ago, if maintenance work was needed, it was possible to simply turn off the supply for homes for a few hours overnight and no one would notice. Now, if the supply cuts out for 30 seconds, everything starts flashing, and the residents have to spend half an hour resetting everything.

Another factor in rising energy use has been the increase in the number of single-person households—the more people who live in a house, the more energy efficient it is because you only need, for example, one washing machine and one central heating system. The average number of people per household has dropped from 2.9 people in 1971 to 2.3 now, as a result of an increase in the number of divorces, longer life spans and the ability of more single people to afford their own homes. Almost 70% of the expected rise in households from 1996 to 2016 can be attributed to single-person households.

The upshot of all of these factors is that personal carbon emissions account for 43% of the total, or about 235 Mt CO_2 a year. Whatever the causes, this rise in energy consumption must be reversed. An 80% reduction in these emissions equates to 18 Mt CO_2 a year. This sounds like an impossibly large amount, and many people see this as a threat to their way of life. But we should be able to meet all of our climate goals without giving that up. It is possible to maintain our lifestyle but use much less high-carbon energy. And although it often seems that only expensive or far-off technological breakthroughs can make a difference, a low-carbon future can be achieved with a combination of existing technology, bold policy decisions and the right personal choices.

Communications equipment and other consumer electronics will continue to proliferate and will outpace the improvement in energy efficiency of each individual device, so we need to be more enlightened.

THE EFFICIENCY IMPERATIVE

A range of measures can be taken. First, it is important to encourage the most efficient products and phase out the most energy-hungry by making it really clear which are the best performers and making that a real feature at the point of sale. This is a process that is already under way, through labels such as the "energy saving recommended label." It is a process that will accelerate as the EU's Directive for Eco-Design of Energy-using Products, which came into force in 2007, begins to feed through into the high street.

More "choice editing" of inefficient appliances—which could include voluntary agreements, price signals or outright bans—would get around the problems of energy ratings by simply ensuring that all household appliances are maximally efficient. It can include setting maximum power levels too, so there's no need for people to agonize over buying decisions or the interpretation of complex labeling.

We also need to give people clear messages so they know how to decarbonize their lives—but without overwhelming them with too much information. And people need to be nudged in the right direction with policies that make it easier to act in a sustainable way and harder to take the high-carbon option. The most effective way to engage people is through the concept of value—low-carbon options can save you money. However, often there is a large up-front cost, so we need the right funding packages in place to allow people to make the choices that are right for the environment and right for them, too.

It is not just conserving energy that we need to tackle—the same approach must be taken to saving water, reducing waste and using resources more sustainably.

CULTURE SHOCK

All the changes brought in by government and the new technologies that are coming on line are not enough. We need changes at a more fundamental level—our attitudes regarding energy must change. The first steps on this road have been taken—since 2008's rapid surge in fuel prices, people have become more aware of energy use, and the advent of the carbon market has for the first time made the fact that there is a price to be paid for carbon emissions explicit.

Using less energy—and water—has to become second nature, and this is an area where smart meters can play a key role because the first step is to give people information about what they are using and how much that costs them. As the technology develops, it will be able to help people make the right choices automatically—turning off appliances when it senses no one is home, for example, and turning on the heating when the residents are on the way home from work.

In time, all homes will be zero-carbon, with many of them generating their own electricity and selling it back into the grid. We will still have as many gadgets as we do now, if not more, but they will be even more efficient, and many functions now done separately by different devices will be consolidated—one device may act as phone, MP3 player, digital camera, video recorder, TV and laptop, for example. Our heating and hot water may be provided by a district heating scheme, cutting costs—and carbon emissions—dramatically.

We will look back at products such as patio heaters and bottled water with amazement that we could ever have used such wasteful goods. We are already seeing signs that sustainability is becoming aspirational—this attitude will spread and become more mainstream.

THE RIGHT PRICE SIGNALS

But to get to this stage, on a broader level we need the right policies to encourage the type of low-carbon generation technologies that can wean us off our dependence on fossil fuels. No one will invest in new plant, whether that is nuclear power, offshore wind or anything else, unless the long-term signals are right because these are long-term investments where it takes 20 years to get a return on investment.

The Climate Change Act, the world's first climate change legislation that was introduced at the end of 2008, has a very long-term target—out to 2050—but there are not enough policy support mechanisms to help us get there. The EU's Emissions Trading Scheme (ETS) is the main policy mechanism, but many people are doubtful that it will provide sufficiently robust long-term signals to get new low-carbon generation. It will be politically compromised by arguments over the allocations to various industries, and it is a relatively short-term mechanism in the context of the life of power stations.

Ideally, we would move on from the ETS to something like a carbon tax, but given where we are now, that would be difficult. The Climate Change Act and the ETS are not going to be sufficient to ensure the investment needed to decarbonize the grid. The market needs to believe that the ETS will endure in its current or a similar form for several decades, and we need something to supplement the ETS, such as a guaranteed floor price that will provide the incentive and the certainty to encourage the industry to build low-carbon generation.

The UK has to deal with the fact that most of the companies expected to invest in new generation capacity are international and have choices about where to put their money. They will only invest in the UK if the market signals are at least as good as elsewhere.

Here, our deregulated market structure is starting to work against us— it was fine when we expected most of Europe to follow suit, but that has not happened. We find ourselves at the western end of a gas market supply chain that stretches all the way back to Russia—making the security of our energy supplies a real concern.

The deregulated system will have to change. There will need to be more prescription and clearer price signals. We need some kind of body that specifies the proportion of energy generated by gas, nuclear and renewable sources, and we can allow the gap to be generated by something else.

The price signals will be helped by the fact that the low oil prices we saw in the early part of 2009 are unlikely to return. New exploration for oil and gas needs a long-term price of about $75 a barrel, so that is likely to be the floor price in the future. This price will also be needed to encourage the building of new refining capacity—if that capacity is not built, we will see big spikes in the price when demand picks up.

It is a sign of how quickly things have changed that, just over a year ago, we would have thought $75 a barrel was a very high price. Having seen prices soar to double that level and then crash to around $30 a barrel, we have a new and probably more realistic perspective about the volatility of energy prices and the havoc this uncertainty can wreak on the world economy. As our imports increase, we will be unable to insure ourselves against this rise in global prices with our own oil exports.

Of course we do not necessarily want to see more oil production; we want to see a decoupling of fossil fuel use and economic growth. However, for that to come about requires a critical mass of low-carbon generation capacity, a big increase in energy efficiency and a reduction in demand.

For the foreseeable future, we will still need fossil fuels to provide baseload power, but we need to decarbonize this as much as we can. At the same time we need to maximize the amount of microgeneration capacity being installed by customers.

The UK's 80% reduction target by 2050 is achievable, but we will need to throw everything at the problem—decarbonizing the grid and using smart meters, smart appliances and the smart grid as well as more established measures such as insulation to make buildings zero-carbon. We need to focus on all the basic boring measures such as insulation, low-energy light bulbs, and efficient appliances before we start thinking about more esoteric solutions.

It is not enough to focus just on the 2050 targets—many scientists believe we have only until 2015 to stabilise emissions—that is a real challenge. In terms of current known technologies, the UK has probably lost the battle to become a world leader. If we are really serious about building a UK technology supply chain, we have to look at investing in next-generation technologies such as carbon capture and storage, fuel cells and marine. However, it also creates real opportunities in areas ranging from humble home insulation and the production and installation of microgeneration to tidal and wave power. Grabbing these opportunities means jobs and business opportunities.

5 Economizing, Innovating, and Sustainable Economic Performance
A Business School Perspective

Christos N. Pitelis and Jochen Runde

INTRODUCTION

The aim of this chapter is to revisit Lionel Robbins's famous definition of economics from a business school perspective and in the light of post-Robbins developments in neoclassical economic theory, evolutionary economics and management scholarship. The thrust of our argument is that while economics in its Robbinsian "economizing" guise contains important lessons for business school audiences, his insistence on economic analysis proceeding by taking means-resources—what he calls the "ultimate data" of "technique" and institutions (such as property rights)—as givens, may actually divert attention from or even obscure various other issues of central importance from a business school perspective. The reason for this is that while business leaders and managers are certainly interested in questions of economizing, they are also interested in questions of innovation and strategy. Many of the issues involved here are ones that have less to do with the efficient allocation of given resources than with addressing questions of how resource constraints might be reduced (i.e., with technological change, increasing returns, intertemporal efficiencies and the productivity-enhancing effects of the co-evolutionary character of market structures, organizations and technological change. These factors are vital determinants of intertemporal efficiency and sustainable economic performance, and therefore cannot be treated simply as parameters that are only interesting insofar as they affect relative scarcities.

The chapter is structured as follows. We begin in the next section by reviewing the definition of economics proposed by Robbins in his 1935 *The Nature and Significance of Economic Science* (henceforth NSES) and argue that his particular view of economics as being purely about economizing is of a piece with his view that economics is not about the causes of wealth or welfare. The section titled "The Economizing Conception and Business School Economics" then looks at the influence of the Robbinsian view on business school economics via post-Robbinsian economic theory. The following section, "Robbins and Technique: Economizing or Innovating?" discusses recent developments in neoclassical economic theory, evolutionary economics and management scholarship that focus on the role of technological change and its relationship to market structures, organizations and institutions. We argue that these developments put into question Robbins's view that the economist should treat "technique" and "institutions" as "ultimate data." In particular, we argue that economizing cannot always be treated as separate from innovating, and that in the business world it is mainly through innovation and technological change that long-term value maximizing can be effected. The final section closes with some concluding remarks.

ROBBINS'S DEFINITION OF ECONOMIC SCIENCE

According to Robbins's famous definition, "Economics is the science which studies human behaviour as a relationship between ends and scarce means which have alternative uses" (Robbins, 1935, p. 16). By "ends" Robbins means human objectives, possible states of affairs that can be can be ranked in terms of their importance or desirability. By "means" he has in mind the resources, including time, that could be deployed to achieve those ends. Economic problems, as he conceives them, arise in situations where there are competing ends of different levels of importance, and where the available means could be put to more than one use and are scarce relative to those ends. In situations of this kind economic choices have to be made:

> when time and the means for achieving ends are limited *and* capable of alternative application, *and* the ends are distinguishable in order of importance, then behaviour necessarily assumes the form of choice. Every act which involves time and scarce means for the achievement of one end involves the relinquishment of their use for the achievement of another. It has an economic aspect. (Robbins, 1935, p. 14)

Robbins thus characterizes economics in terms of what we will call an economizing orientation, namely a concern with analyzing how scarce resources may be put to their best use. He contrasts this conception with what he calls the "materialist" conception that he associates with scholars such as Cannan, Marshall, and even Pareto and J. B. Clark, and according to which economics is about the "causes of material welfare" (Robbins, 1935, p. 4). Robbins is sharply critical of this conception and insists that whatever economics may be about, it is not about the causes of material welfare (Robbins, 1935, pp. 4–23). However, the target of Robbins's criticism is not so much the emphasis on the causes of welfare per se, but that a focus on *material* welfare would render economics unable to accommodate certain activities such as enjoyment of leisure and the services of an opera singer on the grounds that these are not instances of *material* wealth (Robbins, 1935, pp. 4–23).

Robbins is surely right that leisure activities and the provision of services should fall under the purview of economics. As he puts it:

> is true that the scarcity of materials is one of the limitations of conduct. But the scarcity of our own time and the services of others is just as important. The scarcity of the services of the schoolmaster and the sewage man have each their economic aspect . . . it is not the *materiality* of even material means of gratification which gives them their status as economic goods; it is their relation to valuations. It is their relationship to given wants rather than their technical substance which is significant. (Robbins, 1935, pp. 21–22)

However, accepting that the scope of economics extends to "non-material" welfare and the implication that the materialist conception of economics should be rejected for excluding them does not by itself imply that economists should not be concerned with the causes of welfare in some more general sense. That is to say, there is no logical barrier to allowing that economics should be concerned with "economizing" in the Robbinsian sense, at least in part, and also extend to the analysis of causes of welfare. As far as Robbins himself is concerned, and while he is unequivocal in his insistence that economics is not about the causes of material welfare in Chapter I of NSES, he there does not explicitly deny that it might be about the causes of welfare in a more general sense[1].

In Chapter III Robbins goes on to claim that instead of dividing economics into the theory of production and the theory of distribution—where the former is concerned with explaining "the causes determining the size of the 'total product'" and the latter with "the causes determining the proportions in which it is distributed between different factors of production and different persons" (Robbins, 1935, p. 64)—as Adam Smith and others economists did, we now have "a theory of equilibrium, a theory of comparative statics and a theory of dynamic change" (Robbins, 1935, p. 68). Robbins leaves his reader in little doubt about his position on the theory of production:

> We have all felt, with Professor Schumpeter, a sense almost of shame at the incredible banalities of much of the so-called theory of production—the tedious discussions of the various forms of peasant proprietorship, factory organization, industrial psychology, technical education, etc., which are apt to occur in even the best treatises on general theory. (Robbins, 1935, p. 65)

And commenting on Adam Smith's own excursions on this topic:

> although Adam Smith's great work professed to deal with the causes of the wealth of the nations, and did in fact make many remarks on

the general question of the conditions of opulence which are of great importance in any history of applied Economics, yet, from the point of view of the history of theoretical Economics, the central achievement of his book was his demonstration of the mode in which the division of labour tended to be kept in equilibrium by the mechanism of relative prices. (Robbins, 1935, p. 68)

The upshot of all this is that, for Robbins, it is never the ends and means in their own right that are of significance for the economist, only the relationship between ends and means. That is to say, means (and ends) should be treated as givens by economists, as "ultimate data" that it is not their business to enquire into:

> the subject matter of Economics is essentially a set of relationships— relationships between ends conceived as the possible objectives of conduct on the one hand, and the technical and social environment [means] on the other. Ends as such do not form part of this subject matter. Nor does the technical and social environment. It is the relationship between these things and not the things in themselves which are important for the economist. (Robbins, 1935, p. 38)

And again:

> Economists are not interested in technique as such. They are interested in it solely as one of the influences determining relative scarcity. Conditions of technique "show" themselves in the productivity functions just as conditions of taste "show" themselves in the scales of relative valuations. But there the connection ceases. Economics is a study of the disposal of scarce commodities. The technical arts of production study the "intrinsic" properties of objects or things. (Robbins, 1935, pp. 37–38)

THE ECONOMIZING CONCEPTION
AND BUSINESS SCHOOL ECONOMICS

Robbins's view had a revolutionary impact on economics (see, for example, Baumol, 1984), as taught both in economics departments and in business schools. In the case of business schools, much of the economics taught zeroes on what we will call "core" microeconomics delivered in the familiar neo-classical style of standard introductory and intermediate textbooks. While the level and extent of provision varies quite significantly across schools, as well as across different programs offered within the same schools, the kind of topics that tend to be covered invariably include some elementary price theory, the theory of the consumer, the theory of the firm (costs, revenues and profit maximization), market structure, some managerial economics, welfare economics and market failure (market power, externalities and public goods).

Neoclassical microeconomics is widely regarded as the paradigm example of economics in its Robbinsian guise, and this is true of economics texts directed at a business school audience. Thus, UK-based authors Nellis and Parker (2006) in their *Principles of Business Economics* declare that

> Economics is concerned with the efficient allocation of scare resources. When purchasing raw materials, employing labour and undertaking investment decisions, the manager is involved in *resource allocation*. (Nellis & Parker, 2006, p. 3, emphasis in the original)

Similarly, U.S.-based authors McKenzie and Lee (2006), in what is described on the cover as "the first microeconomics text written exclusively for MBA students," distinguish the economist's work from that of other social scientists as follows:

> Economists take a distinctive approach to the study of human behaviour, and they employ a mode of analysis based on certain presuppositions. For example, much of economic analysis starts with the general proposition that people prefer more to fewer of those things they value and that they seek to maximize their welfare by making, reasonable, consistent choices in the things they buy and sell. (McKenzie & Lee, 2006. 10)

While neither book mentions Robbins specifically and McKenzie and Lee display a preference for American over British authorities, the spirit of the Robbins view clearly shines through in the passages quoted above. Further, it seems to us right that business school students be exposed to the economizing perspective in the Robbinsian sense, since business leaders, managers and entrepreneurs are often engaged in allocating resources, in having to make difficult choices between competing ends under conditions of scarcity and attempting to find more efficient and cost-effective ways to perform already-existing functions. Basic lessons about resource allocation, opportunity costs, diminishing returns, marginal analysis and so on are central to all this kind of activity and therefore valuable to the students.

There are of course other reasons for teaching core microeconomics to a business school audience. First amongst these is that it provides a theory of price and insights into the operation of the price mechanism, a characterization of the firm and different forms of market structure and their effects—especially useful with respect to more mature and relatively more stable sectors (Pitelis, 2007)—and the effects of market failure (the last of which is becoming increasingly important because of increasing concerns about the environment and relevant policy responses). Second, microeconomics is in many ways a fundamental discipline that provides the theoretical underpinning of parts of other subjects that students will encounter on their courses, such as business strategy. Michael Porter's (1980) approach to competitive strategy, for example, derives from the microeconomic market structure analysis. Third, a grounding in microeconomics puts students in a better position to receive, interpret and evaluate the many messages they will be receiving about the "economy" during their working lives.

However, to say that the core microeconomics taught in business schools is useful is of course not to say that there aren't limitations to the material and its potential relevance. Some of these limitations are directly related to aspects of the economizing orientation articulated by Robbins, but others have do with features of the discipline that have crystallized in ways that he might not have imagined. Here are three features we regard as characteristic of modern microeconomics and which we shall focus on below:

1. The assumption that actors are motivated purely by self-interest and pursue this aim in a perfectly informed and perfectly consistent way, maximizing utility if they are consumers or maximizing profits if they are firms. In general, the methodology of core microeconomics is to analyze economic phenomena as the outcome of the actions (and interactions of) such rational agents. This approach is consistent with Robbins's conception of economics (Robbins, 1935, p. 78).
2. An emphasis on static allocative efficiency and the idea that this is most likely to be effected by the desirable properties of certain "optimal" market (industry) structures such as perfect competition, perfect contestability or Bertrand competition (see, for example, Varian, 1992). This emphasis is largely a post-Robbins development.
3. A failure to explore the full ramifications of the possibility that industry structures which are optimal from the point of view of static efficiency, may well be sub-optimal from the point of view of dynamic or intertemporal efficiency. This failure reflects Robbins's insistence on treating "technique" as a datum, thereby discouraging the analysis of the determinants of technological change[2].

To appreciate these issues better, it is worth remembering that one of the major achievements of this approach has been to prove that under conditions of perfect competition, a market economy, will allocate (scarce) resources in an efficient way. Economic efficiency is approximated by Pareto efficiency, defined as a situation in which it is not possible to make any one person better off without making someone else worse off. In addition, any Pareto efficient situation can be shown to correspond to a competitive equilibrium, given an appropriate distribution of endowments (see Dasgupta, 1986, for a critical assessment of these ideas).

These are powerful results. However, it is clear that they have been achieved at the cost, not only of narrowing the scope of economics to what we have called an economizing orientation concerned exclusively with the efficient allocation of scarce resources as per Robbins, but also of leading to a largely uncritical view of the virtues of highly idealized "optimal" types of market structures. There has accordingly been a slew of criticisms of this approach, of which we will briefly consider two. In the first place it has been pointed out that its emphasis on self-interest maximization has rendered economics free of any considerations or virtuous behavior (Sen, 1987). Second, the alleged optimality of "optimal" industry structures such as perfect competition and perfect contestability has been questioned. Both of these structures are characterized by the presence of free entry and costless exit by other firms, essential to establishing their "zero waste" property. As Baumol (1991) puts it:

> It is the costlessness of entry and exit under perfect competition or contestability that prohibits all inefficiency, because any firm that indulges in wasteful expenditure cannot long survive the incursion of efficient entrants. (p. 12)

Baumol goes on to show that for this very reason, firms in perfectly competitive or contestable markets will have an incentive to degrade and misrepresent product quality and to also abuse the environment. This will be so even in "repeated games" provided that some players are "transient"[3].

There are related issues in respect of "intertemporal" efficiency. One of the stylized facts of the innovation literature is that it is neither the "midgets" nor the "giants," but rather medium-sized firms that innovate the most. Indeed there is considerable evidence that the relationship between the degree of competition within an industry on the one hand and its innovation performance on the other is of the inverse U-shape-type (see Aghion et al., 2005, for a recent re-statement). Large-sized firms are incompatible with perfect competition, albeit compatible with contestability. However, as Baumol (1991) notes, the conditions of free entry and costless exit deprives firms of the very incentive to innovate, namely Schumpeter's (1942) "transient" monopoly profit. Assuming that innovations are good for sustainable economic performance, ceteris paribus, "optimality" of market structures may be inimical to intertemporal efficiency.

Robbins's conception of economics is more general than core microeconomics as characterized in the three points listed above. One reason for this is that he does not link his definition with ideal market structures that can deliver the efficient allocation of scarce resources. Another and perhaps more important reason is that Robbins is concerned not only with static, but also with dynamic/intertemporal efficiency (see Robbins, 1935, pp. 68, 71, 79, 102–103, and below). Nevertheless, Robbins's definition could lead to some confusion and could be criticized on some counts. We will mention two issues here, before moving on.

First, Robbins seems ambivalent as to the role of "time." He refers to one's time and resources, raising the question whether or not time is a resource. It could be argued that time is the ultimate resource as an individual could not do very much in its absence. In addition, while from the point of view of the individual time is the ultimate scarce resource—there is little one can do to extend it at any given point in time. Over time, it is possible to extend time, both at the individual level (for example through increases in life expectancy) and at the aggregate level (through increases in productivity and the size of the population). This challenges the notion of the amount of time being given and the distinction between resource allocation and resource creation, which we return to below.

A similar point can be made about knowledge. There is an extensive literature on knowledge that points to its "public good" characteristics, as well as its tacit, cumulative-increasing returns aspects (see Polanyi, 1966; Buckley & Casson, 1976; Stiglitz, 1989, and the "endogenous growth" literature, for example, Romer, 1986)[4]. If knowledge is a resource (as argued for example by Marshall, 1961 [1920]), and if it is not scarce, at least not in all cases, Robbins's definition may need reconsidering and the relationship between knowledge, "technique," market structures, institutions and organizations, placed center stage.

ROBBINS AND TECHNIQUE: ECONOMIZING OR INNOVATING?

We have seen that according to Robbins, economics should be conceived as an approach that, beginning with the ultimate data of technology and institutions, and the assumption of rational behavior, is concerned with the efficient allocation of scarce resources. Reflecting on NSE in his Richard Ely lecture in 1981, Robbins (1984) restates these views but allows for what he called "political economy" (as opposed to economic science) to go further than economic science, by affording itself the luxury of becoming involved with issues that require value judgments.

The great advantage of the "modern" approach to theoretical economics, according to Robbins, is that it derives from a number of simple postulates:

> The main postulate of the theory of value is the fact that individuals can arrange their preferences in an order, and in fact do so. The main postulate of the theory of production is the fact that there is more than one factor of production. The main postulate of the theory of dynamics is the fact that we are not certain regarding future scarcities. (Robbins, 1935, pp. 78–79)

Commenting on the apparently static conception of his approach, Robbins suggests that one can use it to analyze dynamics in two ways.

> In the first place, we may compare the equilibrium positions, assuming small variations in the data . . . [and we] may also endeavour to trace out the path actually followed by different parts of a system if a state of disequilibrium is given . . . And in so doing all this we make no assumption that final equilibrium is necessary. (Robbins, 1935, p. 102)

Finally, concerning "technical change and innovation" (Robbins, 1935, p. 133)—which includes "changes in the legal framework" (Robbins, 1935, p. 134)—Robbins asks the question "how can we tell in advance what choice will be made?" (Robbins, 1935, p. 134). Accordingly given such uncertainty "there are certain things which must be taken as ultimate data" (Robbins, 1935, p. 135).

Our own concern in the remainder of this chapter, is to delve a bit deeper into the following issues raised by Robbins. First, can the efficient allocation of scarce resources be separated from resource creation? Second to what extent do "technique" and "institutions" impact not only on relative scarcities but instead co-evolve, thus impacting on technology and resource-creation, and therefore on scarcity, innovation, intertemporal efficiency and macroeconomic performance?

A useful point of departure is Kaldor's (1972) observations on increasing returns to scale:

> When every change in the use of resources—every reorganisation of productive activities—creates the opportunity for a further change which would not have existed otherwise, the notion of an "optimum" allocation of resources when every particular resource makes as great or greater contribution to output in its actual use as in any alternative use—becomes a meaningless and contradictory notion: the pattern of the use of resources at any one time can be no more than a link in the chain of an unending sequence and the *very distinction*, vital to equilibrium economics, *between resource-creation and resource*-allocation loses its validity. The whole view of the economic process as a medium for the "allocation of scarce means between alternative uses" falls apart—except perhaps for the consideration of short-run problems, where the framework of social organisation and the distribution of the major part of available "resources", such as durable equipment and trained or educated labour, can be treated as given as a heritage of the past, and the effects of current decisions on future development are ignored. (pp. 1245–6, emphasis added).

For Kaldor (1972) economic theory went wrong when:

the theory of value took over the centre of the stage—which meant focusing attention on the allocative functions of markets to the exclusion of their creative functions. (p. 1240)

Similar points are made, among others, by Nobel Laureate Douglass North (1981, 1990, 1994). Moreover in contrast to Robbins, Kaldor asserts that the most salient part of Adam Smith's analysis pertains to the productivity benefits deriving from the division of labor through "dynamic economies of scale" (p. 1243) rather than the equilibrating role of markets. The point here is that resource allocation and resource creation may be hard to separate and that whether the creative or allocative functions in markets are most important may well depend on the issue at hand. For example, for issues involving change and economic development (North, 1994), or the growth of firms (Penrose, 1959), a focus on the creative-developmental aspects may be more appropriate than a focus on the allocative ones.

For North (1994), "Neoclassical theory is simply an inappropriate tool to analyze and prescribe policies that will induce development. It is concerned with the operations of markets, not with how markets develop. How can one prescribe theories when one doesn't understand how economies develop?" (p. 359).

For Penrose (1959), moreover, the neoclassical "theory of the firm" "is but part of the wider theory of value, indeed one of its supporting pillars, and its vitality is derived almost exclusively from its connection with this highly developed, and still basically unchallenged, general system for the economic analysis of the problem of price determination and resource allocation" (p. 11). While this theory serves a useful purpose, when "kept in its habitat" (p. 13), "Difficulties arise when an attempt is made to acclimatize the theory to an alien environment and, in particular, to adapt it to the analysis of the expansion of the innovating, multiproduct, 'flesh-and-blood' organisations that businessmen call firms" (p. 13).

With respect to the relationship between technique, institutions and scarcity, a number of authors have suggested that the single most important determinant of the creation of knowledge and innovation in capitalist economies has been the capitalist firm (Penrose, 1959; Chandler, 1962, 1990; Baumol, 1991). Now knowledge is a resource, and one subject to increasing returns (Stiglitz, 1989). Institutions, intertemporal efficiency through increasing returns and resource creation through knowledge and innovation (intertemporal efficiency), are linked in such complex ways, that to assert the exogeneity of technique and institutions may be questionable. Critically, the production of knowledge engenders increasing returns and questions the optimality of "optimal industry structures" such as perfect competition and perfect contestability. This implies that apparently suboptimal industry structures, such as big business competition, as well as non-collusive inter-firm cooperation (Richardson, 1972) may be more "optimal" from the point of view of resource-knowledge creation and (thus) intertemporal efficiency (Schumpeter, 1942; Penrose 1959; Chandler, 1962, 1990; Richardson, 1972; Nelson & Winter, 1982; Baumol, 2002).

The above suggest that both economizing and innovating should be part and parcel of economic analysis, and that reducing the one to the other or placing exclusive emphasis on the one at the expense of other may be unwarranted. Indeed, neoclassical industrial organisation (IO) scholars have spent significant resources in exploring the relationship between market structure and technological change (Baumol, 1991; Scherer & Ross, 1991) apparently disregarding Robbins's advice. More recently whole schools of economic thought dwell on the nature, role and significance of innovation, see Fagerberg, Mowery and Nelson (2005) for a recent account. Some of this work has found its place in leading economics journals, as in the cases of Teece (1977), Dosi (1988), and Nelson and Winter (2002).

In addition and in partial recognition of their importance, some concerns of evolutionary economists and management scholars (such as increasing returns, knowledge spillovers, the importance of human capital and technological change) as well as the endogeneity of innovation have more recently been recognized by endogenous growth theorists (e.g., Romer, 1986; Lucas, 1988) and scholars of comparative institutions (such as Richardson, 1972; Williamson, 1985) and economic history such as Douglass North (1990, 1994). As already noted, the problem of some such scholars departs from Robbins in some important ways (see Stiglitz, 1989; North, 1994).

To conclude, institutions and technique can affect relative scarcities, as well as the very vehicles (such as market structures) that we rely on in the study of economics. In this context considering them as data, outside the scope of economic analysis, may well unduly restrict the scope of the subject. The work of and indeed Nobel Prizes to Ronald Coase (1937, 1960) and Douglass North (1981, 1990, 1994), who used transaction cost analysis to explain the firm and the law (Coase) and economic development (North), attest to that. In addition technical change impacts on (and is affected by) (optimal) market structures, making it difficult to explore the one by taking the other as datum. Importantly, one could well be justified to question even the direction of causality. For example Schumpeter (1942) and more recently the leading neoclassical scholar Harold Demsetz (1972) suggest that it is superior innovative capability (Schumpeter), or "differential efficiency" (Demsetz), that determine firm size and industry structure. Put simply, it may be innovation and efficiency that cause market structure, not the other way around. How interesting that Demsetz has used his view as a critique of the mainstream structure, conduct, performance model of IO!

In the past 30 years or so, business scholars responded to increasing demands by students and business people alike to understand not just the economizing aspects of modern capitalist firms but also its strategizing and innovating elements, by drawing on neoclassical, transaction costs, resource-based, evolutionary and behavioral views, such as those of Coase (1937), Schumpeter (1942), Penrose (1959), Cyert and March (1963) and Nelson and Winter (1982). The result is some fascinating work on the co-evolution of institutions, organizations, technological change, transaction costs, resources and (dynamic) capabilities, and market structures and sustainable economic performance; see for example Nelson and Winter (2002) and Fagerberg et al. (2005)[5]. In a surprising turn, the neoclassical market structure analysis has been used by Porter (1980) to develop a "strategizing" (rent extraction through monopoly power) approach to business strategy. Others, notably Oliver Williamson (1991) lamented this development, putting emphasis on economising, albeit in transaction (not production) costs. The resource-based and dynamic capabilities views, have brought production costs back in (see Penrose, 1959; Richardson, 1972; Wernerfelt, 1984; Barney, 1991; Peteraf, 1993; Teece, 2007). The "systems of innovation" view drew on the work of Schumpeter (1942), Nelson and Winter (1982) and others to focus on the innovating aspects of organizations and institutions, and market structures. None of these makes any value judgments and/ or interpersonal comparisons of utility, such as those that would lead Robbins to exclude them from positive economic science on this basis. With notable exceptions (such as Coase, Williamson and North), no genuine inroads into mainstream economics have been made from such approaches. This is despite the ultimate recognition by the profession of many such scholars. Perhaps the time has come for the discipline to embrace such contributions. As originally noted by Robbins, it seems to us that it is not a waste of time to attempt this, but "a waste of time not to do so" (Robbins, 1935, p. 3).

CONCLUDING REMARKS

Reflecting on his original essay in his Richard T. Ely lecture of 1981, Robbins reiterates his view that economics should be about "economizing" and that "technique" and "institutions" should be viewed as ultimate data. This view has been highly influential in the development of neoclassical economic theory. What has been added since Robbins is the modern emphasis on the construct of optimal market structures as vehicles for achieving static Pareto efficiency. It is this second feature, in our view, that has led neoclassical economics astray in some important respects, not least in encouraging a limited understanding of the relationship between market structure and intertemporal efficiency.

Post-Robbins developments in neoclassical economic theory, notably in IO, and endogenous growth theory depart from the Robbins's tradition of conducting economic analysis on the assumption that "technique" can be treated as a given. In so doing they acknowledge the importance of concerns of evolutionary, Schumpeterian "systems of innovations" and management scholars, who have traditionally emphasized the important role of innovation and technological change, not merely in influencing relative scarcities but also in affecting market structures and firm, industry, resource creation and macroeconomic performance. The contributions of scholars such as Coase, Demsetz, Chandler, North and Stiglitz, have helped to add legitimacy to such concerns.

From the perspective of business, and business school scholarship, economizing, strategizing and innovating are equally valid and interrelated concerns. Building on the work of economists such as those mentioned above, business school scholarship has developed some fascinating accounts of the co-evolution of markets, resources, knowledge, innovation, institutions, and firm and industry structures as well as sustainable economic performance. From a business school perspective treating "technique" and "institutions" as data is limiting, perhaps even boring. Perhaps the time is ripe to consider wealth creation and its key determinant (technological change and innovation) as legitimate concerns of neoclassical economics, too.

NOTES

1. Indeed one may be forgiven in thinking that Robbins would not disagree with this when he states that "The services of the opera dancer are *wealth*. Economics deals with the pricing of these services, equally with the pricing of the services of a cook" (Robbins, 1935, p. 9, emphasis added). Robbins, however, goes on to say that economics should not, nevertheless, be concerned with the determinants of the wealth of nations. This may strike his readers as somewhat inconsistent.
2. Robbins does not focus on optimal industry structures. Credit for exploring the link between market structure and technological change (or intertemporal efficiency) is due to neoclassical industrial organization scholars who have attempted to test the so-called Schumpeterian hypothesis (see Baumol, 1991). With a few exceptions, however, notable amongst whom is Baumol, they have subsequently failed to explore the relationship between optimal market structures, static efficiency and intertemporal efficiency.
3. The performance of such market structures will instead be better in the case of another aspect of virtuous behavior, that of racial, sex or other forms of discrimination. "Zero waste" suggests a tendency against discrimination, but here too the outcome is not always guaranteed (Baumol, 1991).
4. For Stiglitz (1989, p. 198), "Among the 'commodities' for which markets are most imperfect are those associated with knowledge and information. In many respects, knowledge is like a public good. Firms may have a difficult time appropriating their returns to knowledge, resulting in an undersupply; and to the extent that they are successful in appropriating, underutilization results (since they will have to charge for its use)."
5. Note, however that it is far too risky to refer to particular references here, as the work amounts to many hundreds of articles published in journals such as *Academy of Management Review, Organisation Science* and *Strategic Management Journal*. Even a cursory look at any recent issue of these journals would suffice to confirm our claim.

REFERENCES

Aghion, P., Bloom, N., Blundell, R., Griffith, R., & and Howitt, P. (2005), Competition and innovation: An inverted-U relationship. *Quarterly Journal of Economics*, 120, 701–28.

Barney, . (1991). Firm resources and sustained competitive advantage. *Journal of Management*, 1, 17, 99–120.

Baumol, W. J. (1984). Foreword. In *An essay on the nature and significance of economic science* (3rd ed.). London: Macmillan.

——(1991). *Perfect markets and easy virtue*. Oxford: Blackwell.

——(2002). *The free-market innovation machine: Analyzing the growth miracle of capitalism*. Princeton, NJ: Princeton University Press.

Buckley, P. J., & Casson, M. (1976). *The future of multinational enterprise*. London: Macmillan.

Chandler, A. D. (1962). Strategy and structure: Chapters in the history of the industrial enterprise. Cambridge, MA: MIT Press.

——(1990), *Scale and scope: The dynamics of industrial capitalism*. Cambridge, MA: The Belknap Press of Harvard University Press.

Coase, R. H. (1937). The nature of the firm. *Economica*, 4, 386–405.

——(1960). The problem of social cost. *Journal of Law and Economics*, 3, 1–44.

Cyert, R. M., & March, J. G. (1963). *A behavioral theory of the firm*. Englewood Cliffs, NJ: Prentice Hall.

Dasgupta, P. (1986). Positive freedom, markets and the welfare state. *Oxford Review of Economic Policy*, 4, 25–36.

Demsetz, H. (1972). Industry structure, market rivalry, and public policy. *Journal of Law and Economics*, 16, 1–9.

Dosi, G. (1988). Sources, procedures, and microeconomic effects of innovation. *Journal of Economic Literature*, 26, 1120–71.

Fagerberg, J., Mowery, D., & Nelson, R. R. (Eds.) (2005). *The Oxford handbook of innovation*. Oxford: Oxford University Press.

Kaldor, N. (1972). The irrelevance of equilibrium economics. *The Economic Journal*, 82, 1237–55.

Lucas, R. E. (1988). On the mechanics of economic development. *Journal of Monetary Economics*, 22, 3–42.

Marshall, A. (1961 [1920]). *Principles of economics* (9th ed.), C. W. Guillebaud (Ed.). London: Macmillan.

McKenzie, R. B., & Lee, D. R. (2006). *Microeconomics for MBAs: The economic way of thinking for managers*. Cambridge: Cambridge University Press.

Nellis, Joseph G. M. and Parker, David (2006), *Principles of business economics*, 2nd edition, Harlow: Pearson Education Limited.

Nelson, R. R., & Winter, S. G. (Eds.) (1982). *An evolutionary theory of economic change*. Cambridge, MA: Belknap/Harvard University Press.

——(2002). Evolutionary theorising in economics. *Journal of Economic Perspectives*, 16, 12, 23–46.

North, D. C. (1981). *Structure and change in economic history*. New York: Norton.

——(1990). *Institutions, institutional change, and economic performance*. Cambridge: Cambridge University Press.

——(1994). Economic performance through time. *The American Economic Review*, 84, 359–68.

Penrose, E. T. (1959). *The theory of the growth of the firm* (3rd ed.). Oxford: Oxford University Press.

Peteraf, Margaret, A. (1993). The cornerstone of competitive advantage: A resource based view. *Strategic Management Journal*, 14, 479–88.

Pitelis, C. N. (2007). Market-based theory. In S. R. Clegg & J. R. Bailey (Eds.), *International encyclopaedia of organization studies* (vol. 3. pp. 876–881). Sage.

Polanyi, M. (1966). *The tacit dimension*. London: Routledge and Kegan Paul.

Porter, M. E. (1980), *Competitive strategy*. New York: The Free Press.

Richardson, G. (1972). The organisation of industry. *Economic Journal*, 82, 883–96.

Robbins, L. (1935). *An essay on the nature and significance of economic science* (2nd ed.). London: Macmillan.

Romer, Paul M. (1986). Increasing returns and long-run growth. *Journal of Political Economy*, 94, 1002–38.

Scherer, F. M., & Ross, D. (1991). *Industrial market structure and economic performance* (3rd ed.). Boston: Houghton Mifflin Company.

6 Green Values in Communities
How and Why to Engage Individuals with Decarbonization Targets

Michael Pollitt

INTRODUCTION

It is a great pleasure to offer this paper as a contribution to the "Green Values and Green Business" colloquium organized by the Centre for International Business Administration & Management (CIBAM). As usual CIBAM have managed to pick a topic which poses a significant but as yet unresolved challenge for the business community. This Chapter is an attempt to discuss some of the ethical issues associated with climate change and to emphasize one important way forward toward a solution.

The substantial decarbonization of the global economy required by an effective climate change policy has at its heart some highly debateable ethical assumptions. If anything the ethical challenges raised by climate change are even greater than is generally acknowledged. There is a general assumption that macro-level policy will be able to achieve decarbonization at reasonable financial cost and with limited impact on lifestyles. However this is unlikely to be the case, with a clear trade-off between higher financial costs and lesser behavioral impacts on lifestyles.

Instead, we need a much more open and honest discussion of the significant likely financial and lifestyle costs of tackling climate change. We suggest that engaging individuals and changing norms of behavior will be crucial if decarbonization is to be achieved and if the full costs of climate change and related development challenges are to be willingly met by democratic societies around the world. Engaging individuals and changing norms fundamentally relate to individual moral values. This brings us to a consideration of how organized religion can play a role in providing the moral basis for individual action in this area. We also suggest how business will need to engage with the challenges posed by decarbonization.

The chapter is organized in five sections. The second looks at the ethics behind the recent Stern Review on *The Economics of Climate Change* (Stern, 2007) which makes the case for early action on decarbonization. The third section examines how individual ethics and behavior can be changed to meet climate change policy targets. The fourth looks at the implications for company behavior of these ethical changes, and the final section is a conclusion.

ETHICS AND THE STERN REVIEW

The Stern Review, initially published in 2006, was a UK Treasury-sponsored document produced by a team of civil servants led by Lord Nicholas Stern. It was an important document in providing a basis for UK policy toward climate change and in laying out a case for early action on decarbonization. It laid the basis for the Climate Change Act 2008 which sets a binding commitment to reducing UK carbon emissions by 80% of 1990 levels by 2050. Under the Climate Change Act the UK now produces five-year carbon reduction budgets, recommended by the Committee on Climate Change, which set targets for keeping the UK economy on track to achieve its 2050 targets. The first three draft budgets were published in late 2008 (Committee on Climate Change, 2008). The government is legally required to take policy action to ensure that the UK is on track with its carbon budgets. The recent annual government budget included a substantial discussion of policy measures shaped by the Committee's recommendations (see HM Treasury, 2009). The Stern Review has partly inspired international discussions on a "Global Deal" on climate change which formed an important input into the UN climate conference in Copenhagen in late 2009. Indeed, in subsequent work Lord Stern clearly lays out the suggested elements of a Global Deal in the light of the original Stern Review (see Stern, 2008a, 2008b).

The Stern Review was noteworthy partly because it focussed on the *economic case* for *early* action on decarbonization. In contrast to much earlier economic work it suggested that the social cost of a tonne of CO_2 (and other greenhouse gases—GHGs) produced now was much higher than previously calculated. This calculation lies behind its call for deeper cuts in GHG production sooner rather later. In broad outline, the Stern Review suggested the cost of climate change under a business as usual trajectory could rise to 5% of world GDP per annum (with a significant chance of costs up to 20% of world GDP), while the cost of mitigating GHG reduction was around 1% of world GDP per annum, if we started to invest now. At the real social discount rate assumed in the Review (1.4%), this implies a strongly positive net present value (NPV) of action.

Critics of the Review focused their discussions on the calculation of the social discount rate, on which the case for early action turns. According to the theory of social discounting (see Evans, 2008):

$$SDR = r + e.g$$

SDR = social discount rate

r = pure rate of time preference

e = inequality aversion parameter

g = growth rate of consumption per head

r is a measure of extinction risk (i.e., the extent to which future generations will be around to enjoy the benefits of investments made now). It reflects the risk that human civilization may disappear and hence it is not worth making social investments at the expense of current consumption.

e reflects societal preferences toward inequality across and between generations. A lower value implies we care less about inequality in the sense that we would prefer to make investments rather than simply transfer current consumption. Thus, low discount rates driven by this parameter mean more investment, less current consumption and more current inequality.

g is a measure of economic growth. Higher expected growth rates mean that future generations will be richer than the current one, and hence for given preferences toward inequality, society should be less willing to reduce current consumption to improve the wealth of future generations.

For many studies (see Weitzman, 2007) a common assumption is that *r* = *g* = 2% and *e* = 2. This implies SDR = 6%.

The Stern Review assumes that *r* = 0.1%, *g* =1.3%, *e* =1. This implies SDR = 1.4%.

Thus, the Stern Review assumes that global society faces a low extinction risk (*r*). The low inequality parameter (*e*) implies that we don't care that much about inequality (though we do care somewhat). The low growth rate parameter (*g*) assumes much lower levels of world GDP growth than in the recent past. The overall implication is that we are happier than previously assumed to transfer consumption to future generations and we care less than previously about dealing with current inequality.

The underlying ethical assumptions implicit in the 1.4% discount rate have been severely criticized on a number of fronts. Nordhaus (2007) points out the inconsistency between this discount rate and the discount rates used in earlier economic analyses of climate change for which a higher discount rate (in the region of 6%) has been typical. Dasgupta (2007) highlights a fundamental problem with a low inequality parameter, which is that it implies much more saving for the future than we actually observe. Dasgupta suggests that setting *e* = 1 might suggest we should be saving up to 97.5% of our GDP to invest in social projects with positive returns in the future. Dasgupta's ethical point is that doing something about climate change at the same time as not doing much about global poverty implies ethically questionable value judgments. Rich Westerners are prepared to reduce their consumption now to save their own children's children but are not prepared to reduce their consumption now to save poor nations' children now. This echoes the arguments of Lomborg (2001) who suggests that there are more pressing threats to global development (such as tackling HIV in Africa) than climate change.

Weitzman (2007) makes a rather different point about the use of discount rates. He suggests that the Stern Review may have arrived at the right answer by the wrong method. For him the key problem is uncertainty. The introduction of uncertainty about future growth rates, including the introduction of the possibility of negative growth rates leads to much lower values of the discount rate than 6% even if *e* = 2 and *r* = 2%. It is also the case that with "fat tails" in the distribution of climate impacts such that the probability of extremely negative GDP outcomes remains significant (rather than tending to zero as in a normal distribution), then the discounted damages may be extremely large even at higher discount rates. The appropriate way of handling such uncertainty is via purchasing catastrophe insurance which argues for early action on decarbonization to reduce the probability of extremely negative outcomes (arising from very high temperature rises).

Other criticisms have been leveled at the calculations of the costs of climate change by Carter et al. (2006). They argue that the Stern Review was systematically biased in its use of scientific evidence on climate change and made use of the most pessimistic scenarios of the temperature impacts of anthropomorphic carbon emissions. Byatt et al. (2006) upon examining the cost and benefit calculations in the Review suggest that it combines pessimistic scenarios as to the climate impact and economic cost of climate change with optimistic scenarios for the cost of mitigation (i.e., low costs). They also suggest that it ignores an earlier more skeptical report by the House of Lords Select Committee on Economic Affairs (2005). Neumayer (2007) makes a rather different criticism pointing out that the Stern Review assumes the substitutability of financial and natural capital. Neumayer argues that assuming non-substitutability of the two types of capital would be a better assumption (and would also support early action to stop natural capital loss).

Indeed, to suggest the cost of mitigation could be as low as 1% of world GDP rather obscures the likely true cost. As Dasgupta (2007) points out, this becomes 1.8% of the GDP of developed countries, if they have to bear all of the cost (which seems likely initially). If one assumes optimism bias in the costing of mitigation projects, this could double the cost (given that many involve large capital cost programs or high transaction costs). If one further assumes that many of the least-cost responses, while technically possible, are not implemented and adjustment is required by second best means, then costs could easily be doubled again. Given that the difference in the cost of their budget programs between the two main political parties seeking election in advanced democracies is usually of the order less than 0.5–1% of GDP, a policy which could ultimately cost of the order 5% of GDP is one which will require a significant individual engagement with and belief in it. This is especially true given the fact that keeping the overall cost down requires high actual or implicit transfers from rich to poor countries which are likely to be significant as a percentage of rich countries GDP. The development aid budgets of rich countries are currently a small fraction of 1% of GDP. Therefore, it is clearly a leap of faith to assume that all developed countries will necessarily be willing to spend large sums solving global climate problems rather than adapting their own economies to the reality of climate change as it emerges.

Stern (2008a) robustly responds to his critics. He recognizes the need to include uncertainty in calculating the discount rate, but argues that this lowers it. He acknowledges and defends the role of his low assumptions of *r* and *e*. He suggests that it is easy to justify a discount rate in the range of 1.5–5%. In a further paper (Dietz et al., 2008) he (and his co-authors) recognize that standard market economics as embodied in the social discount rate is not enough to handle the values of society with respect to climate change. Stern (2009) goes further suggesting that discounting cannot adequately handle the climate problem and that taxes are only part of the solution. He suggests that changed individual attitudes have a role to play in reducing the cost of public policy (p. 33): "The more that people take on board damages to others, through discussion and information, and worry about them directly, the less need for other public policy actions."

Stern (2008a) contains a summary of his suggestions for the key elements of a Global Deal on Climate Change (which are expanded in Stern, 2008b) to put the size of the flows of payments from developed to developing countries to pay for carbon reduction activity. The size of total aid flows from developed to developing countries is currently of the order of $100 billion.

Targets and Trade:

- 50 percent cuts in world emissions by 2050 with rich country cuts at least 75 percent.
- Rich country reductions and trading schemes designed to be open to trade with other countries, including developing countries.
- Supply side from developing countries simplified to allow much bigger markets for emissions reductions: **"carbon flows" to rise to $50–$100 billion per annum by 2030.** Role of sectoral or technological benchmarking in "one-sided" trading to give reformed and much bigger CDM (Clear Development Mechanism) market.

Funding Issues:

- Strong initiatives, with public funding, on deforestation to prepare for inclusion in trading. For $10–15 billion per annum could have a programme which might halve deforestation. Importance of global action and involvement of IFIs (International Financial Institutions).
- Demonstration and sharing of technologies: e.g., $5 billion per annum commitment to feed-in tariffs for CCS (Carbon Capture and Storage) coal could lead to 30 new commercial size plants in the next 7–8 years.
- Rich countries to deliver on Monterrey and Gleneagles commitments on ODA (Official Development Assistance) in context of extra costs of development arising from climate change: **potential extra cost of development with climate change upward of $80 billion per annum.**

(Stern, 2008, p.31)

Box 6.1 The Suggestions for a Global Deal on Climate Change

The size of the program envisaged under the Global Deal is clearly substantial. However, while the Stern Review focuses on global ethical assumptions, there are important additional distributional issues between nations when it comes to how the burden should be shared between them. While developed countries might accept the principle of converging on the same level of emissions per head across all countries (taking trading into account) by 2050, this neglects the fact that this implies inequality in the cumulative emissions per head taking into account emissions history since the industrial revolution (see Johansen, 2007). Even to achieve equity in the final per head emissions target the United States might need a 90% cut in GHG emissions by 2050 (which is a much more severe relative cut than any other major country). Developing countries might find it difficult to neglect the issue of taking cumulative emissions into account, especially as it is cumulative emissions that cause global warming.

The policy challenge posed by the need to decarbonize the world economy is huge. The costs to individuals within advanced economies are likely to be noticeable and significant. They will require rises in the price of energy, transport and energy-intensive goods to finance supply-side changes to production methods (or to purchase offsetting emissions reductions abroad). They will also imply significant demand-side response in terms of shifting consumption to less-energy-intensive goods and associated behavioral change (e.g., using public transport more often). They will also require individuals to support investments which have significantly higher global benefits than national benefits, and may often be located abroad. This will require society within developed countries, such as the UK, to actively support the policies that are required to achieve the goal of decarbonization over a long period.

The recent failure of the UN climate conference in Copenhagen to reach a Global Deal has only illustrated the difficulties that many countries will have in implementing the drastic cuts in emissions required. Given that the probability of a self-enforcing international agreement to promote radical action is currently low, this further emphasizes the need for increased "grassroots" pressure for climate policy to create sufficient political motivation for action.

INDICIVIDUAL VALUES, BEHAVIORAL CHANGE AND EFFECTIVE CLIMATE CHANGE POLICY

In this section we argue that individual values are important in achieving decarbonization of the economy and that it is important to understand how these values are formed can be influenced.

Von Storch and Stehr (1997, p. 90) provide a helpful framework for thinking about the way that climate policy comes about. They suggest that while it is true that climate policy is notionally based on the optimization of welfare (as in the Stern Review), there are two important filters through which the calculation of welfare maximization has to go. First, there are the "interpreters of climate"—who are the "experts" who evaluate the information that we have on the climate. In our age we might see these as mainly being scientists, such as those represented by the UN International Panel on Climate Change (IPCC). Von Storch and Stehr (1997) have a nice illustration from the Middle Ages of the role of Church in interpreting the meaning of series of bad-weather-induced poor harvests in Europe in the years 1315 to 1319. The Church interpreted the lack of agricultural productivity caused by unfavorable weather as a judgment from God and called on the people to repent. Second, there are the "interpretative systems of society" which determines what the "costs" of adaption and abatement are and also defines the welfare function that is being optimized. Thus, the interpretative system might hear what the scientists have to say and actually think that the lifestyle changes required to abate carbon are too high and the benefits too uncertain. What is clear from this framework is that "climate science" and indeed "economic science" do not determine climate policy, they *merely* inform it. Societal values are the ultimate determinant of climate policy. Different societies and different individuals receiving the same scientific information will come to different conclusions on the actions (if any) to be taken. Recent controversies about the reliability of climate science following the revelations about the alleged manipulation and withholding of climate data by a prominent university research department only highlights the political sensitivity of climate policy to the filtering process through which it passes.[1]

Tjernstrom and Tietenberg (2008) look at how individual values relate to national climate policy. They used International Social Survey Program data on 8000+ respondents from 26 countries for the year 2000. They found that national emissions reductions targets were higher in countries where a higher percentage of individuals think that climate change is important and where there is higher press freedom and higher trust in government. Individuals were more likely to think that climate change was important if they were better educated, lived in an urban area and had more affinity with other countries. The authors conclude (p. 323) that "what citizens believe does matter" for policy.

Vandenburgh, Barkenbus, and Gilligan (2008) discuss the role of the individual in taking action on carbon emissions in the United States. They outline seven actions which would have a significant overall impact on U.S. emissions. These include reducing idling of cars, reducing the use of standby power and maintaining the proper tire pressure. Even assuming limited uptake, the total expected emissions reduction from these individual actions could be 7% of U.S. residential and domestic emissions. Vandenburgh et al. (2008) discuss the process by which we get individuals to change their behavior. They argue that regulation alone is unlikely to work (or even to get enacted). Raising prices (e.g., of gasoline) would be an obvious economic policy, but this has serious distributional consequences, especially in the short term. In the absence of effective regulation or high enough prices it is necessary to appeal to a moral imperative to get individuals to change their behaviour. What is needed is "personal norm activation" (i.e., a spontaneous change of behavior created by a sense of duty in the absence of explicit sanctions) (Vandenburgh, 2005). The sorts of norms that will be important in encouraging individuals to take actions to curb carbon emissions are those of "environmental protection," "personal responsibility" (for the climate problem), and "reciprocity" toward individuals in developing countries (and other places) who will bear the brunt of the costs of a changing climate. Personal norm activation is closely related to the need to "inspire," to "win hearts and minds" and to "instil strong personal and moral values" in the area of environmental responsibility.

The need for personal norm activation suggests that we need to turn to 'norm' specialists (see Johnson, 2008). The most obvious places to turn for help (globally) in this area are religious institutions (such as Christian churches). Religious institutions activate norms regularly in their role of interpreting what God may be saying in this generation. They have had an honorable role in many of the most momentous norm changes in society: the civil rights movement, the environmental justice movement, third world debt relief and the collapse of the Iron Curtain. Recently in the United States for instance almost all major Christian denominations have expressed strong support for sustainable development and for decarbonization, and indeed changing public attitudes in the United States to taking action on climate change reflect the clear stances of the churches on this issue.

Of course, there is a debate about whether religion is good for the environment. Lynn White (1967) drew attention to the "creation ordinance" in Genesis 1:28 as the Judaeo-Christian justification for exploitation of the natural world and the religious support for industrialization and the massive growth of economically motivated exploitation of national resources, of which carbon emissions are merely one consequence. However, in reality religion has played a more mixed role (see Berry, 2006). The sustainable development movement traces its intellectual origins back to a Christian philosopher—Rev. Thomas Malthus—who first warned about the likely limits to human exploitation of natural resources (see Mebratu, 1998). The econometric evidence on the impact of Christianity on attitudes to environment is weakly positive (for 1993) in the United States (see Boyd, 1999). However, for the UK evidence (for 1993) suggests that overall affiliation to a Christian denomination makes no difference to attitudes regarding the environment, although educational attainment and scientific knowledge about the natural environment are significant and there are some differences between denominations (see Hayes and Marangudakis, 1999). Similar results are found for a 1993 sample covering the United States, Canada, Great Britain and New Zealand (Hayes and Marangudakis, 2000). Pepper,

Jackson, and Uzzell (2010) find that adherence to Christianity has a positively significant, if small, impact on socially conscious and frugal consumer behavior for a sample of UK consumers.

Examination of the key religious texts of the three great monotheistic
religions—Judaism, Christianity and Islam—shows that they all provide
strong support for care of the environment.[2]

Judaism: "The heavens declare the glory of God; **the skies proclaim the
work of his hands.** Day after day they pour forth speech or language where
their voice is not heard. Their voice goes out into all the earth, their words
to the ends of the earth." (Psalm 19: 1–4)

Christianity: "The creation waits in eager expectation for the sons of
God to be revealed. For the creation was subjected to frustration, not by
its own choice, but by the will of the one who subjected it, in hope that **the
creation itself will be liberated from its bondage to decay** and brought into
the glorious freedom of the children of God." (Romans 8: 19–21)

Islam: "The sun and the moon to a reckoning, and the stars and trees
bow themselves; and heaven—He raised it up and set the balance. **Trans-
gress not in the balance, and weigh with justice, and skimp not in the balance.**" (Sura 55: 5–9)

As with previous religious inspirations for behavioral change, connections between taking action and the central tenets of religious faith
need to be highlighted and recognized as being important *for now.* It
seems to be that science is telling us that the time is coming for action
on climate change. It is increasingly clear that only if connections are
made with personal norms of behavior that the required (radical) action
will be forthcoming. For many people (even if they are not religious) a
religiously inspired movement may be the only way to bring about the
scale of behavioral change that is required via both individual action and
individual example. The challenge is that climate change is clearly an
international development problem involving actions by and in developing countries. Helping developing countries develop poses conventional
challenges which remain difficult or impossible to solve. For example
changing incentives within developing countries with rain forests to
incentivize their continuation is not just a matter of climate policy but of
conventional economic development. However, as all the great religions
emphasize, rather than worrying about the action/inaction of others we
should start by changing our own actions.

Sandelands and Hoffman (2008) lay out the key role for religion in
tackling climate change very clearly. They note that encouraging people
to take action on climate change will only work if environmental sustainability is seen as part of a true sustainability. Individuals are not motivated
by economic social cost-benefit analyses, what they need is an appeal to
their "hunger for meaning." As Fromm (1977, p. 137) puts it: "Only a
fundamental change in human character from a preponderance of the having mode to the predominantly being mode of existence can save us." The

Global Deal will founder if it is ultimately merely based on an economic analysis of the climate problem. What is needed is an engagement of the mass of individuals in advanced countries (and eventually in developing countries) in a movement toward a more sustainable world. As Sandelands and Hoffman (2008, p. 13) suggest, this will require a desire to help others across borders and be based on a politics which is based on hope rather than fear. This is because if people lose hope that meaningful decarbonization can be achieved (because of a lack of trust in their own and other countries' governments), then it will never be achievable, as a lack of belief will give rise to a self-fulfilling prophecy.

It is important to point out that the suggestion that religiously inspired changes in personal behavior and attitudes are likely to be important in tackling climate change only highlights of difficulty of bringing about radical action on climate. Indeed in Pepper, Jackson, and Uzzell's (2009) survey of consumer attitudes in Woking, England, highlighted that a reduction in consumerism (or an increase in frugality) was only significantly impacted by a personal motivation to frugality or a reduction in income. Adherence to organized religion is on the decline in many Western countries (though not in many rapidly developing ones), and religious institutions are inherently conservative and subject to the same sorts of obstacles to behavioral change as the individuals who support them (Douglas & Pepper, 2009). Douglas and Pepper suggest that what is needed is a "green" religion that combines the personal environmental commitment of non-institutional eco-spirituality (in some New Age movements) with the significant transformative social and community movements born out of organized religion. In this way positive personal attitudes to the environment might be translated into support for effective action. The issue is how to harness both the considerable power of organized religion to bring about social change (by engaging committed adherents *and* other people of goodwill) in order to win hearts and minds to the considerable behavioral changes and economic costs required in tackling climate change.

This view is supported by Pope Benedict in his 2009 letter *Caritas in Veritate* or "Charity in Truth."[3] This thoughtful document highlights the difficulty of global economic development in the absence of a truly integral humanism. It addresses, among other things, the need to address global environmental problems and recognize the "covenant between human beings and the environment" (para. 51). The Pope concludes: "Openness to God makes us open towards our brothers and sisters and towards an understanding of life as a joyful task to be accomplished in a spirit of solidarity. On the other hand, ideological rejection of God and an atheism of indifference, oblivious to the Creator and at risk of becoming oblivious to human values, constitute some of the chief obstacles to development today" (para. 78). In other words, religion can help us to overcome our indifference to the plight of others and to tackle global development problems, such as climate change, rather than to focus on our own personal and local self-interest.

IMPLICATIONS FOR COMPANIES

Companies can help or hinder the accumulation of institutional, relational, moral and spiritual capital in society as constituent parts of their total impact on social capital (Heslam, Jones, & Pollitt, 2009). Firms build institutional capital by adhering to the laws of the country and supporting legitimate authority. Firms build relational capital by having strong stakeholder relationships internally and externally. Firms build moral capital when ethics are embedded in core business operations and when accountability structures are put in place that will keep the moral dimensions of the company's core operations under review and in development as new ethical challenges emerge. Firms exhibit spiritual capital when they pay attention to their "soul," articulate and develop their—and by implication their employees—sense of ultimate purpose, and have strategies to ensure that this is shared throughout the company. All of these types of social capital building by firms will be needed to address issues of environmental sustainability.

These four capitals will each be shaped by the sort of world which is engaged with climate change policy. Responsible large, and particularly multinational, companies will be increasingly impacted and required to respond in its attitude to how it builds social capital. Thus, *institutional capital building* by firms will involve participation in emissions trading schemes, standards and adherence to environmental laws as facts of life. Firms should comply with these schemes and be responsible in their lobbying toward (against?) them. *Relational capital building* will bring firms increasingly into contact with a post-materialist (see Inglehart, 1990) and personal environmental norm activated world. Both customers and employees will expect firms to take decarbonization seriously. *Moral capital building* will require companies to have values and set examples which actively promote environmental sustainability. All companies, but particularly multinationals, should demonstrate integrity, consistency and transparency of actions toward the environment. *Spiritual capital building* will require companies to have an inspiring vision about why the company exists and what drives it, *other than* the quest for profit. This will be because society will/should increasingly recognize that participation in this sort of vision is central to its survival.

Companies will need to support and respond to the personal norm activation of employees and customers, and to some extent participate in it. A good example of this is the UK High Street retailer, Marks and Spencer's Plan A[4]. This is a comprehensive set of commitments to a whole range of environmental targets, including carbon reduction, aimed at responding to and anticipating rising consumer sensitivities.

CONCLUSIONS

The economic case for early decarbonization is highly debatable, with a financial social cost-benefit analysis capable of being subjected to a wide range of criticisms which make the use value of such analysis for policy questionable. However, the moral case for early action on the grounds of environmental sustainability and economic and environmental justice is overwhelming.

It is undeniable that the costs of decarbonization will be substantial and involve a significant political cost. Even if the cost were only 1% of world GDP per annum, this would involve much higher costs in advanced countries, historically large international transfers to developing countries and significant redistributional consequences between sectors and individuals within advanced countries.

The current vision for action is narrowly focussed on the scientific case for convergence in emissions per head by 2050. This raises major ethical issues to do with historical emissions and the conflicts between the environment and development within developing countries. The slow progress toward a Global Deal on climate change only highlights the difficulty and vulnerability of effective climate policy and the requirement to gain and maintain active public support for decarbonization.

We have argued that we need to seriously engage with ethics, morality and religion in tackling environmental issues. Individual behavior will need to change, and there will need to be significant individual engagement with the climate change issue in order to ensure support for the expensive international policies that are required. If we do not engage in this sort of personal norm activation there is no chance we will meet the targets suggested by climate scientists. In parallel, companies will increasingly be called on to support the building the sort of institutional, relational, moral and spiritual capital that supports climate change action.

NOTES

1. See, for example, Ben Webster and Jonathan Leake (2010, January 28), Scientists in stolen e-mail scandal hid climate data, *The Times*, Retrieved from http://www.timesonline.co.uk/tol/news/environment/article7004936.ece. Accessed February 2, 2010.
2. For some good resources on religion and the environment, see http://daphne. palomar.edu/calenvironment/religion.htm. Accessed February 2, 2010.
3. Available at www.vatican.va/holy_father/benedict_xvi/encyclicals/documents/hf_ ben-xvi_enc_20090629_caritas-in-veritate_en.html. Accessed February 2, 2010.
4. See http://plana.marksandspencer.com/. Accessed February 2, 2010.

REFERENCES

Berry, S. (2006). Is religion bad for the environment. *The Bible in Transmission*, Summer, 1–6. Available online at http://www.biblesociety.org.uk/uploads/ Products/product_123/TransMission_-_Sustainable_developement_Summer_2006_-_Is_religion_bad_for_the_environment.pdf

Boyd, H. H. (1999). Christianity and the environment in the American public. *Journal for the Scientific Study of Religion, 38*, 36–44.

Byatt, I., Castles, I., Goklany, I. M., Henderson, D., Lawson, N., McKitrick, R., Morris, J., Peacock, A., Robinson, C., & Skidelsky, R. (2006). The Stern Review: A dual critique, Part II: Economic aspects. *World Economics, 7*, 199–229.

Carter, R. M., de Freitas, C. R., Goklany, I. M., Holland, D., & Lindzen, R. S. (2006). The Stern Review: A dual critique, Part I: The science. *World Economics, 7*, 167–98.

Committee on Climate Change (2008, December 1). *Building a low-carbon economy - the UK's contribution to tackling climate change*. Norwich: TSO. Available online at: http://www.theccc.org.uk/pdf/TSO-ClimateChange.pdf

Dasgupta, P. (2007). Commentary: The Stern Review's economics of climate change. *National Institute Economic Review, 199*, 4–7.

Dietz, S., Hepburn, C., & Stern, N. (2008). Economics, ethics and climate change. In K. Basu and R. Kanbur (ed.) *Arguments for a Better World: Essays in Honour of Amartya Sen* (Vol. 2: Society, Institutions and Development), Oxford: Oxford University Press, pp. 365-386.

Douglas, S., & Pepper, M. (2009). Is "green" religion the answer to the ecological crisis? A reflection in the context of the English-speaking West. In Datta Banik, S. & S. K. Basu (Eds.), *Environmental Challenges of the 21st Century*. New Delhi: A.P.H. Publishing.

Evans, D. (2008). Social project appraisal and discounting for the very long term. *Economic Issues, 13*, 61–70.

Fromm, E. (1977). *To have or to be*. London: Continuum.

Hayes, B. C., & Marangudakis, M. (1999). Religion and attitudes towards nature in Britain. *British Journal of Sociology, 52*, 139–55.

———(2000). Religion and environmental issues within Anglo-American democracies. *Review of Religious Research, 42*, 159–74.

Heslam, P.S., Jones, I.W. and Pollitt, M.G. (2009), *How a social capital approach can help multinationals show ethical leadership*, University of Cambridge, mimeo.

HM Treasury (2009, April). Budget 2009 - Building a low carbon economy: implementing the Climate Change Act 2008. London: HM Treasury. Available online at: http://webarchive.nationalarchives.gov.uk/+/http://www.hm-treasury.gov.uk/d/Budget2009/bud09_carbon_budgets_736.pdf.

House of Lords Select Committee on Economic Affairs (2005). *The economics of climate change, Vol.1: Report; Vol.2 Evidence*, London: The Stationary Office.

Inglehart, R. (1990). *Culture shift in advanced industrial society*. Princeton, NJ: Princeton University Press.

Johansen, I. (2007). *Ethics of climate change: Exploring the principle of equal emission rights*. Norwegian Academy of Technological Sciences, NTVA.

Johnson, S. M. (2008), *Is religion the environment's last best hope? Targeting change in individual behaviour through personal norm activation* (Working Paper, Mercer University Law School).

Lomborg, B. (2001). *The skeptical environmentalist: Measuring the real state of the world*. Cambridge: Cambridge University Press.

Mebratu, D. (1998). Sustainability and sustainable development: Historical and conceptual review. *Environmental Impact Assessment Review, 18*, 493–520.

Neumayer, E. (2007). A missed opportunity: The Stern Review on climate change fails to tackle the issue of non-substitutable loss of natural capital', *Global Environmental Change, 17*, 297–301.

Nordhaus, W. (2007). A review of the Stern Review on the economics of climate change. *Journal of Economic Literature, 45*, 686–702.

Pepper, M., Jackson, T., & Uzzell, D. (2009). An examination of the values that drive socially conscious and frugal consumer behaviours. *International Journal of Consumer Studies, 33*, 126–36.

————(2010). Christianity and socially conscious and frugal consumer behaviors. *Environment and Behavior.* Published online before print October 19, 2010, doi: 10.1177/0013916510361573.

Sandelands, L. E., & Hoffman, A. (2008). *Sustainability, faith and the market* (Ross School of Business Working Paper Series, No. 1107).

Stern, N. (2007). *The economics of climate change.* Cambridge: Cambridge University Press.

————(2008a). The economics of climate change. *American Economic Review,* Papers and Proceedings, *98,* 1–37.

————(2008b). *Key elements of a global deal on climate change.* London: London School of Economics.

————(2009), *Imperfections in the economics of public policy, imperfections in markets, and climate change.* Presidential Lecture for the European Economic Association, Barcelona.

Von Storch, H., & Stehr, N. (1997). Climate research: The case for the social sciences. *Ambio, 26,* 66–71.

Tjernstrom, E., & Tietenberg, T. (2008). Do differences in attitudes explain differences in national climate change policies. *Ecological Economics, 65,* 315–24.

Vandenbergh, M. P. (2005). Order without social norms: How personal norm activation can protect the environment. *Northwest University Law Review, 99,* 1101–66.

Vandenbergh, M. P., Barkenbus, J., & Gilligan, J. (2008). Individual carbon emissions: The low-hanging fruit. *UCLA Law Review, 55,* 1701–58.

Weitzman, M. (2007). A review of the Stern Review on the economics of climate change. *Journal of Economic Literature, 45,* 703–24.

White, L. (1967). The historical roots of our ecological crisis. *Science, 155,* 1203–7.

7 Green Business and Green Values
A Perspective from Government

Elizabeth Anastasi

KEY MESSAGES

- Perceptions and expectations of what constitutes green economic activity and employment vary widely.
- All businesses across all sectors of the economy will increasingly have to measure and modify their carbon footprints.
- Demand for low-carbon and environmentally aware business solutions is expected to grow strongly over time. These solutions will become increasingly important in day-to-day business operations.
- Increased requirements for carbon and wider environmental monitoring and reporting necessitate the embedding of climate change risks and future carbon emissions profiles in business investment decisions.
- There is evidence of increased demand-side and supply-side pressures for businesses to accurately signal the green credentials of their products and processes to the market.
- Credible markets are fundamental to addressing many of these issues but may not be sufficient to deliver social optimal outcomes in the long-term public interest due to the presence of market failures and barriers to change.
- The government's primary response to the challenge of removing carbon from economic activity and addressing other environmental impacts has been to create a policy and regulatory framework to provide clear and long-term signals to industry to help shape operational and investment decisions, principally through participation in the EU Emissions Trading Scheme and the Climate Change Bill which commits the UK to statutory targets for emission reductions.
- Given the need to improve environmental performance, the Low Carbon Industrial Strategy aims to ensure that the UK is well-positioned to benefit from the business opportunities with making the transition to a low-carbon economy.

The growing challenges of climate change, both in terms of the need to adapt to the unavoidable impacts of existing environmental damage and to mitigate against further change, mean that "business-as-usual" is no longer an option. Low-carbon, environmental and green concerns more generally should not be addressed in isolation to other economic objectives. These challenges present the need for a fundamental transition to a more sustainable future in the way we live and work. This chapter discusses the potential role for government in facilitating this transition by identifying barriers which may prevent the market from working effectively and where government intervention can help limit these.

PROBLEMS OF DEFINITION: WHAT DOES GREEN ACTUALLY MEAN?

Perceptions and expectations of what it is to be green vary widely across consumers, businesses and countries. In addition, views of what it means to be a green consumer or a green company have changed over time. Definitions have expanded from the use of relatively mature "environmental" technologies associated with pollution clean-up, waste management and recycling, to encompass the development and use of renewable energy technologies, such as electricity generation from wind, wave and tide. In particular, the use of nuclear power has gained greater prominence as a low-carbon technology.

With the increasing urgency attached to tackling climate change, the definition appears to have broadened much further over recent years, covering a wide variety of activities, technologies and sectors, ranging from the creation of more energy-efficient building and low- or zero-emission methods of transportation to the increasing scale and scope of carbon and environmental management and monitoring services, and carbon finance. There has also been a growing focus of the wider environmental and social impacts of businesses' activities through the rise in prominence of corporate (social) responsibility.

The legal commitment by the UK to reduce carbon emissions by 80% by 2050 in the Climate Change Act 2008 demonstrates that the government is committed over the longer term to actions that reduce carbon emissions. The scale of the target will, as outlined earlier, require a fundamental shift in the way all activities are carried out in the UK—leading to a transformation of the industrial landscape and adjustments across the whole supply chain. Businesses across all sectors of the economy will have to increasingly account for their carbon footprint and therefore will, to some extent, have to green their operations. *"A green economy will be one in which lower carbon and resource efficiency will permeate all products and services throughout the entire economy"* (Ernst & Young, 2008).

Legal requirements to account for environmental impacts, including forward-looking legislation such as the Climate Change Act and the establishment of market frameworks such as the European Union Emissions Trading

Scheme, imply that the labels "green" and "not green" will become less meaningful. Instead, products and processes will increasingly become differentiated by "shades of green" as businesses modify the scale and scope of their activities to improve their environmental and social performance alongside their economic objectives.

The United Nations Environment Program (UNEP) recently discussed this spectrum of green activity in the context of distinguishing a number of trends of how employment could change over the wider economy in a "green" transition (UNEP, 2008):

- *Additional jobs will be created*—for example the manufacture of pollution-control devices and new cleaner technologies;
- *Some employment will be substituted*—for example shifting from fossil fuels to renewables or from land filling and waste incineration to recycling (i.e., a shift between sectors or between subsectors);
- *Certain jobs may be eliminated without direct replacement*—for example if packaging materials are discouraged and their production is discontinued; and
- *Many existing jobs will simply be transformed and redefined as day to day skill sets, work methods and job profiles and greened*— in particular, plumbers, electricians, metal workers and construction workers.

This breakdown and the example definition from Ernst & Young quoted earlier help to establish the breadth and depth of what will be required to establish a green economy, spanning a wide spectrum of skills and occupational profiles. The challenge for government is to identify, within this wide range of activities, the barriers that are preventing the market from delivering optimal decisions with respect to the full impacts of their activities and, more importantly, to distinguish where government intervention may be required.

THE DEVELOPMENT OF A LOW-CARBON AND RESOURCE-EFFICIENT ECONOMY

At present, much of the focus of the "green business" discussion focuses on climate change and, within that, the need to significantly reduce the carbon intensity of the way that economic activity is undertaken.

Recent analysis commissioned for the former Department for Business, Enterprise and Regulatory Reform (BERR, now Department for Business, Innovation and Skills, BIS) from independent consultants Innovas and Kmatrix adopted a wide definition of a Low Carbon and Environmental Goods and Services (LCEGS) sector—this definition includes traditional environmental goods and services, renewable energy activities and "emerging low-carbon." Using this definition, the analysis estimates that the global LCEGS sector was worth around £3 trillion in 2007/2008. Of this the UK's LCEGS sector accounted for over £106 billion (roughly 3.5% of the global market and placing the UK sixth in terms of market size) and was estimated to employ around 880,000 people (Innovas, 2008a). The estimates are higher than earlier figures given the broader range of activities captured by the analysis and also because they capture wider supply chain activities in this sector.

The UK emerging low-carbon subsector contributed around half of the estimated market value and employment in the LCEGS sector. In addition, around half of the total market value of the sector was attributed to activity in the supply chain, highlighting the far-reaching implications of the growth in this sector. Demand for low-carbon and environmentally aware business solutions is expected to continue to grow strongly over the coming years as these solutions become increasingly important in the day-to-day business operations across the economy. It is estimated that the UK LCEGS sector grew by approximately 4% in 2007/2008, and, despite the economic downturn, forecasts for future growth of this sector continue to be reasonably buoyant, at over 4% per annum to 2014/2015 (Innovas, 2008b).

Business opportunities in the green economy will not necessarily just accrue to growth of new sectors. Ernst & Young (2008) identified a number of key sectors and subsectors that could develop green business opportunities where the UK already holds a comparative advantage: software, electronic equipment, machinery equipment, financial services[1] and business services[2]. In some cases, the importance of these areas is in terms of the final good or service offered; for others, the importance lies in facilitating the "greening" of operations along the supply chain and as "enabler" technologies, such as information and communication technology (ICT) facilitating the uptake of greener business solutions.

Ensuring that the necessary investment is delivered in a timely way to support the development of such sectors and technologies is clearly important if the UK and other countries are to make a cost-effective transition to a low-carbon economic base, while providing businesses with maximum opportunity to capitalise on future low-carbon business opportunities.

The financial services sector has already taken advantage of the move to more comprehensive pricing of some environmental impacts of economic activity—the pricing and trading of carbon in particular has grown substantially over recent years as governments have sought to establish a credible long-term market framework to allow companies to internalize the environmental costs of their economic activity in the most cost-effective way.

Despite the economic crisis, the global carbon market continued to grow in 2008, with total value of transactions at the end of the year reaching approximately €86 billion—double its 2007 value. Transactions and derivatives under the EU Emissions Trading Scheme (ETS) contributed about

€63 billion to this total, with London benefiting considerably from the development and growth of this market and establishing itself as a world center for carbon trading (World Bank, 2009).

Between 2004 and 2007, global investment in sustainable energy increased substantially year on year, with an average annual growth rate of over 65%. Total sustainable energy financial transactions were valued at $205 billion, with new investment into the sector accounting for around $148 billion of that total (UNEP/SEFI, 2008). In spite of the economic crisis, new investment into the sector rose to $155 billion in 2008, although investment in the second half of 2008 was 17% lower than the first half (UNEP/SEFI, 2009).

To ensure that the UK moves to a more sustainable growth path, it is important to ensure that the economy builds on existing strengths and that businesses take advantage of the economy-wide opportunities arising from the transition. However, despite the progress already made, and the potential for future progress, there appear to be some barriers in the market that are holding back the development of the green economy.

THE RISE IN IMPORTANCE OF CORPORATE RESPONSIBILITY AND ACCOUNTING FOR THE RISKS OF CLIMATE CHANGE

Increased requirements for carbon and wider environmental monitoring necessitate the embedding of climate change risk and future carbon emissions profiles of technologies and business into all investment decisions. Recent analysis from the Carbon Trust (2008) suggests that the implications of climate change for company value would be widely varied across sectors. Some sectors could be expected to gain value (for example, consumer electronics or building insulation), while others would need to transform their activities to maintain or improve company value (for example, aluminium and automotive sectors). Essentially the headline findings suggested that better incorporation of the risks and opportunities for climate change by a well-positioned, proactive company had the potential to increase company value by up to 80%. In contrast, if a company is poorly positioned, or lacking in action in this area, the report suggested that up to 65% of its value could be threatened.

The Government's recent Corporate Responsibility Report (HMG, 2009) outlines a clear business case suggesting that although businesses are legally obliged to make profits, there is scope for improving company performance and shareholder value, improving a firm's profits and working toward competing successful in global markets by going beyond what the law requires. The report demonstrates that corporate responsibility can achieve this impact through both direct links (such as improved efficiency through the reduction or better management of waste, and better risk management) and indirect routes (primarily through building trust and confidence and a increased value from improved reputation).

Despite growing interest in the risks and opportunities of climate change to investors, a recent report for Ceres and the Environmental Defence Fund, suggested that many of the world's leading corporations are failing to provide a full account of the risks and potential costs of climate change (Corporate Library for Ceres and the Environmental Defence Fund, 2009). However, some companies are undertaking activity to monitor and report on environmental impacts and carbon footprints. For example, the Carbon Disclosure Project (CDP) provides information for over 530 institutional investors with assets of over $64 trillion on the carbon performance of some of the largest companies around the world, with a view to improving information flow in the marketplace for investors who are becoming increasingly interested in carbon footprints and the implications of climate change. Their recent report Global 500 publication suggested that reporting companies accounted for close to 6% of total global emissions, when considering direct emissions from their activities. The report suggests improved response rates to the CDP survey and better quality responses reflect the greater corporate engagement and interest by shareholders in climate change. Of respondents to the survey, 74% stated that they had carbon emission reduction targets in place (PWC, 2008, for CDP).

In addition to specific initiatives such as the CDP, increasing interest in greener values is reflected in the rise in the number of market indices, investment funds and individual companies offering investment opportunities that take account of, for example, clean technology and climate change, sustainable development and corporate social responsibility. For example, HSBC's Climate Change Benchmark Index tracks the stock market performance of key companies that are best placed to profit from challenge of climate change. At its launch in 2007 this index had outperformed the MSCI World Index by around 70% when tracked back to 2004 (HSBC, September 2007). Similarly, RBS/ABN Amro's Climate Change and Environmental Index looks at businesses involved in tackling adverse effects of climate change and mitigating environmental degradation. The FTSE Group have also launched an Environmental Markets Index as one of their responsible investment tools.

A growing number of indices also measure the performance of companies in that meet particular corporate responsibility standards. Examples include the FTSE4Good Index (launched in 2001) and the Dow Jones Sustainability Index (launched in 1999), which focus on companies that meet globally recognized corporate responsibility standards and those that are driven more by sustainability issues. Similarly, Business in the Community (BiTC)'s Corporate Responsibility (CR) Index, launched in 2002, attempts to capture the extent to which CR is integrated into day-to-day operations and corporate strategy. Research looking at the link between good performance on CR and financial performance indicators (such as shareholder return and dividend yield) suggested that in addition to demonstrating a correlation with reduced volatility, companies that consistently participated in the CR Index outperformed the FTSE 350 on total shareholder return by between 3.2 and 7.7% per year between 2002 and 2007 (Business in the Community, 2008).

In some cases firms can signal their green credentials to potential customers through participating in initiatives such as the Carbon Disclosure Project or striving for inclusion on one of the market indices as mentioned earlier. However, outside the requirements of the legislative and regulatory framework that businesses operate under, there has been growth in the adoption of voluntary standards and labeling to which firms can aim to get accreditation, and hence signal more easily the credentials of their products.

Aside from a number of products for which minimum standards are enforced, many of the labels currently in use in the marketplace are not formally regulated, as there is no formal requirement at present to meet such criteria. However, some firms strive to adhere to particular British (BSs) or International Standards (ISOs) on, for example, energy management, social responsibility, carbon footprinting and environmental protection. Accreditation to these formal standards and other green or eco-labels requires a firm to meet particular criteria before the standard can be used as part of their marketing and hence signaling to the market. One important aspect of this behaviour is that it not always targeted at final consumers—for companies in the supply or value chain, accreditation to particular standards are useful for signaling environmental or green credentials to potential industrial consumers that are perhaps more sustainably minded.

Consumer decision making has a key role in the development and success (or not) of new goods or services, with well-informed consumers helping to promote competition between firms through switching expenditure to products that more accurately reflect their needs. Increasing consumer awareness of social and environmental issues is creating an incentive in the market for firms to signal directly the carbon content and potential environmental benefits of their products and organizations.

Alongside forecast estimates for the size of the potential markets for greener goods and services, such as those mentioned earlier, survey evidence suggests that customers are showing increasing awareness of the wider impacts of the products that are available to them, and believe there will be increasing pressure on companies to address issues relating to climate change and sustainable development (Ipsos MORI, 2007; PriceWaterhouseCoopers, 2008). One recent survey suggests that consumers were on average willing to pay a premium of around 20% for environmentally and ethically friendly everyday items (PriceWaterhouseCoopers, 2008).

IDENTIFYING BARRIERS TO THE
DEVELOPMENT OF THE GREEN ECONOMY

The government's primary response to the challenge of reducing carbon from economic activity and addressing other environmental impacts is to create a regulatory framework that facilitates open and competitive markets, providing longer-term regulatory certainty for economic agents. However, it is recognized that while credible markets are a necessary fundamental base for addressing many of these issues, they may not be sufficient to automatically deliver outcomes that promote long-term public interest.

Key market failures may affect the ability of the market to deliver optimal solutions, through distorting price signals and incentives or establishing barriers to the creation of a low-carbon, more resource-efficient, greener economy. Externalities (both positive and negative), information asymmetries and significant uncertainty can prevent markets from identifying and taking up the most cost-effective means of addressing and preventing environmental damage.

In his Review of the Economics of Climate Change (2006) Lord Stern stated that climate change was "the biggest market failure that the world has seen." He concluded that the costs of inaction far outweighed the costs of early coordinated international action.

The full social costs of greenhouse gas emissions from economic activity are not automatically internalized by individual economic actors. Private individuals do not take account of the additional costs to society from the actions that they take. Without the internalization of these external costs, private actors will not face the right incentives from the marketplace to properly account for their wider impacts and, where necessary, amend their behavior.

Similarly, the full benefits to society may not be taken properly into account if private actors make investments to address environmental damage already undertaken or to prevent future harm. Failure to take account of these positive spillovers could lead to underinvestment by the market in, for example, supporting infrastructure, R&D and the skills base of the workforce.

At an extreme some goods may not be provided at all—so-called "public goods" which are non-rival and non-excludable[3], such as clean air, in particular suffer from the free-rider problem whereby each individual actor will wait for others to make the decision and then take advantage of any investment made without contributing to the cost.

In addition to the market failure of externalities, information asymmetry and uncertainty can mean that markets may deliver inefficient solutions, since market participants may lack the information they require to make the "right" production or consumption decisions. Similarly, uncertainty, particularly when looking over the longer term, can result in commitment problems—firms may be reluctant to invest in new technologies (in either their development or purchase) if future levels of demand and prices are uncertain. Again, this can lead to underinvestment in innovative activity that could prevent the development of more efficient markets. Commitment problems and uncertainty over the longer term are of particular importance of the context of moving to a greener economy given concerns over losing competitive edge, the difficulties in gaining global commitments on action and the uncertainty over the extent of change that companies will have to adapt to.

Consumer behavior is unlikely to change sufficiently to drive demand for more sustainable and environmentally friendly products if the relevant information that allows them to make informed decisions between products is not easily available. This applies to both final consumers and industrial consumers who may be part of wider supply chains. Industrial consumers that cannot easily access information that will enable them to take up more environmentally sound business solutions may find that there are negative knock-on effects for their own competitiveness. For example, measures to improve the energy efficiency of production processes and buildings can have direct cost savings that mean that companies are able to compete more effectively on the market.

Small and medium enterprises (SMEs) in particular appear to face challenges associated with obtaining adequate information, for example through the lack of capability (time or human resources) to identify better options for carbon reduction actions. In addition to helping companies make better decisions in the short term, better information provision about abatement potentials also reduces some of the uncertainty over the longer term, allowing firms to take a longer-term view when considering investment decisions. This has implications for investment in skills, innovation and infrastructure.

Significant investment in innovation and the necessary skills will be vital for the UK and other countries to make the necessary cuts in carbon emissions in the most cost-effective way and in a timely manner. As such, market failures which lead to underinvestment in these areas (whether from lack of internalization of the true costs and benefits, or problems with information in the market) could severely hamper efforts to reduce environmental impacts and adapt to damage already incurred.

Given the potential for market failures, without government intervention, it is unlikely that private market forces alone will deliver a socially optimum market equilibrium.

GOVERNMENT ACTIVITY IN PROMOTING GREEN BUSINESS AND GREEN VALUES

Government's approach to helping to make the transition to a more sustainable economic growth path needs to take account of relevant drivers of change, such as consumer behavior, the cost of carbon, innovation and regulations to ensure that a credible and consistent regulatory and policy framework is developed over the longer term. Alongside commitments to maintaining macroeconomic stability and a competitive market framework, the government's principal methods of signaling a long-term commitment to reducing carbon is the statutory target to cut greenhouse gas emissions by 80% from their 1990 baseline by 2050 (as outlined in the Climate Change Act 2008) and commitment to the EU ETS. Providing more certainty to markets over the longer term and establishing a market price for carbon help give increased certainty of demand for low-carbon goods and services.

In addition to specific legislation on addressing environmental impacts and carbon emissions reductions, other regulations also have implications for improving wider company performance in areas such as corporate responsibility. For example, the Companies Act 2006 is expected to deliver benefits to business of around £250 million a year (DTI, March 2005). The act contains key provisions relating to directors' general duties and the Business Review that will make a significant contribution to Corporate Responsibility. Part of the statutory statement of directors' general duties establishes the concept of "Enlightened Shareholder Value," which recognizes that, by paying appropriate attention to wider matters, directors will be more likely to achieve sustainable success over the longer term, for the benefit of their shareholders. Similarly, requirements under the Business Review were expanded[4] so that quoted companies must now report on environmental, employee, social and community matters, to the extent necessary to understand the business.

The establishment of regulatory frameworks, such as those which establish carbon pricing and markets for trading of carbon, may go some way to ensuring that the right incentives are in place for companies to take better account of the wider impacts of their economic activities. They are supported by government initiatives that seek to ensure that the necessary supporting infrastructure is in place—this includes direct and indirect investment and support for innovative activity, skills and physical infrastructure.

However, such market mechanisms alone may still not be sufficient to deliver necessary outcomes of improved environmental performance.

In the context of reducing carbon emissions, standard marginal abatement cost (MAC) curve analysis by organizations such as the Climate Change Committee suggest that there are a wide range of carbon abatement options available for take-up. The analysis suggests that although many of these options require a positive carbon price in order to incentivize their development and take-up by the market, others do not. These "negative-cost" measures should not require a positive carbon price, or even necessarily the establishment of a carbon market for their take-up to be cost-effective. Many energy efficiency measures, such as those for improving the building stock or the fuel efficiency of cars, fall into this category. Poor uptake of some of these options suggests that there are perhaps additional failures or barriers in the market, such as those outlined earlier. For example, poor information about the benefits of uptake, poorly aligned incentives or problems with accessing finance to undertaking options that are perhaps more capital intensive.

Government therefore needs to be able to identify what these potential barriers are and, where possible, limit their impact so that the transition to a more sustainable and greener economy can be achieved in the most cost-effective way. There is a wide range of policies targeted at minimizing failures and barriers in the market—actions to improve environmental performance of markets can, to some extent, be considered as a subset of wider policies addressing similar market failures in other areas.

The UK government launched the UK Low Carbon Industrial Strategy in July 2009, alongside the publication of the UK Low Carbon Transition Plan, the Renewable Energy Strategy, and the Low Carbon Transport Strategy. These documents set out a clear vision for a low-carbon future for the UK and seek to provide more certainty about government commitment over the longer term to reduce carbon emissions. The aim of the Low Carbon Industrial Strategy is to ensure, within the context of the requirements to dramatically reduce carbon emissions, that the UK economy is well positioned to take advantage of the potential economic opportunities of a transition to a low-carbon economy. Building on the commitments of earlier policies, these strategies seek to address some of the continuing barriers to a cost-effective transition, and include announcements on the support the research, development and deployment of low-carbon technologies, access to finance for companies such as SMEs that may not be able to find the necessary capital to support viable business proposals and the need to improve information about the opportunities available reducing carbon footprints.

Government has a key role in facilitating the provision of relevant information that may help individual and industrial consumers properly embed the environmental consequences of their choices into their decision-making processes. There are currently a number of demand-side initiatives designed to encourage consumers to think more about implications of their choices. For example, the cross-government Act On CO_2 campaign (launched in 2007) aimed to help businesses and individuals reduce their carbon emissions.

This may include helping to address information failures through helping the supply-side improve the measurement and labeling of the environmental impacts of their products. Government advisory services, such as BusinessLink and the Manufacturing Advisory Service, have a vital role in providing information to business on issues such as energy and resource efficiency, waste, pollution control, and requirements to meet criteria for accreditation to relevant standards.

The UK Low Carbon Industrial Strategy announced a package of initiatives as part of the drive to help SMEs understand the implications of the necessary transition to a low-carbon economy. This included efforts to improve awareness of the opportunities and risks relating to a move to a low-carbon economy, helping SMEs to reduce their carbon footprint and develop low-carbon products.

Binding or voluntary product standards can help address two fundamental market failures through reducing the negative externalities of products and process by driving down the environmental impacts of goods and services and, as highlighted earlier, improve market transparency by increasing the provision of relevant information. British or international standards help improve market transparency across international borders. Further, minimum standards can ensure that demand is focused on a set of goods and services that better take account of the social implications of consumption of these products. However, despite their useful role, it is important to not overstate the impact that standards can play in creating more sustainable products and processes—there is the potential for negative feedback effects on the level of innovative activity undertaken as firms could potentially focus their efforts on developing a reduced number of technologies and products, reducing consumer choice (BERR, 2008).

Government also has an important role to play in driving markets forward through public procurement. The public sector can exert significant buying power in a number of markets on both capital expenditure and current consumption and, hence, by acting as an intelligent customer, play an important role in facilitating the development of new products and processes, for example in markets for clean technology and green products and services. For example, the government's Sustainable Development Strategy commits departments to reduce carbon and waste from their supply chains and public services and to increase water efficiency. These commitments will necessarily affect the way that departments undertake public procurement and ensure that wider sustainability concerns are better accounted for.

In terms of delivering wider objectives on corporate responsibility both in domestic and international markets, the government is responsible for delivering a variety of policies that have an impact on this area. This includes, for example, policies aimed at reducing poverty and disadvantage, as well as promoting human rights both internationally and at home, and involvement in programs such as the Ethical Trading Initiative (ETI) and the International Fairtrade Labeling Organization (FLO). In addition, government supports a wide range of individual sectoral initiatives that provide support to businesses operating in different sectors which are designed to provide businesses with a framework for responsible operations internationally.

NOTES

1. Financial services include investments in carbon trading, carbon offsets, green or clean tech indices and socially responsible investment funds, providing capital for investment in clean technology and environmental products/projects.

2. Business services include environmental consultancy services and environmental marketing.
3. This means that consumption by one does not reduce availability of that good for others, and that it is not possible to effectively exclude particular agents from using the good.
4. All businesses, other than small businesses, were already required to produce a business review prior to the introduction of the Companies Act 2006. The review is prepared by companies for the benefit of their shareholders to help with their assessment of how the performance of the directors.

REFERENCES

BERR (2008). Regulation and innovation: Evidence and policy implications (Economics Paper No. 4).
BIS (2009a), *UK Low Carbon Industrial Strategy.*
BIS (2009b), BIS Economics Paper 1: Towards a Low Carbon Economy – economic analysis and evidence for a low carbon industrial strategy.
Business in the Community (2008), *The Value of Corporate Governance: The positive return of responsible business.*
Carbon Trust (2008). Climate change: A business revolution.
Corporate Library for Ceres and the Environmental Defence Fund (2009). Climate risk disclosure in SEC filings.
DTI (March 2005), *Company Law Reform.*
Ernst & Young (2008). Comparative advantage and green business.
HMG (2009). Corporate responsibility report.
HMT (2006), *Stern Review: The Economics of Climate Change.*
HSBC (25th September 2007), *Press Notice: HSBC launches climate change benchmark index*
Innovas (2009a). Low carbon and environmental goods and services: An industry analysis.
———(2009b). Update of growth forecasts.
Ipsos MORI (2007). Tipping point or turning point?
PricewaterhouseCoopers (2008) for Carbon Disclosure Project 2008, *Global 500 Report.*
PriceWaterhouseCoopers (2008). Sustainability: Are consumers buying it?
UNEP (2008). Green jobs.
UNEP/SEFI (2008). Global trends in sustainable energy investment 2008.
———(2009). Global trends in sustainable energy investment 2009.
World Bank (2009), *State and trends of the Carbon Market 2009.*

8 Sustainability of Corporate Profit

Jack Keenan

BACKGROUND

The Centre for International Business & Management (CIBAM) and Judge Business School presented a February symposium on Green Business and Green Values in February 2009.

CORPORATE GOVERNANCE

Whilst many speakers focused on sustainability, I was asked to look at sustainability of a different sort—the sustainability of a corporation's profit. And, because of a prior CIBAM paper published in *Corporate Governance* (Keenan, 2004), I decided to look at the current or potential role of the UK's Combined Code of Governance in providing profit sustainability for UK-based companies.

I reviewed the UK Combined Code and recalled my own time as an executive board member and later as an independent non-executive. The UK Combined Code today is the sum of several reports and reviews undertaken by leading businessmen beginning with the Cadbury Report in 1992 and finishing with the Higgs Review and Smith Report in 2003.[1]

Today, in light of large-scale value destruction in the UK banking system, there are many calls for another look at the UK Combined Code. My point of view is that the Code today sets out principles and requirements that if properly complied with would have averted levels of profit loss witnessed over the past two years.

The Code tells companies that they must comply with its requirements or explain why they have not. Too many executives and boards claimed compliance without proper procedures and execution. In other words, true compliance had not been achieved, but no explanation was forthcoming.

CORPORATE RISK ASSESSMENT

The key to profit sustainability in the Code lies in the area of internal control and risk management. Specifically in the Principle (D.2) and Provision (D.2.1):

Principle D.2 of the Code states that "the board should maintain a sound system of internal control to safeguard shareholders' investment and the company's assets."

Provision D.2.1 states that "The directors should, at least annually, conduct a review of the effectiveness of the group's system of internal control and should report to shareholders that they have done so. The review should cover all controls, including financial, operational and compliance controls and risk management."

The Higgs Review in January 2003 added to the Combined Code "Suggestions for Good Practice." Importantly, Higgs asked, "What has been the board's contribution to ensuring robust and effective risk management?"

AN EFFECTIVE RISK MANAGEMENT MODEL

The Higgs Review does not actually spell out a model for robust and effective risk management, so at the Cambridge Symposium I spelled out a process that has proven to be effective for several companies to achieve a measure of profit sustainability. There are three pieces to any effective risk management model:

1. Identify key risks
2. Quantify the risks and their probability
3. Mitigate the risks

I believe that the risk management process should be overseen by a company's internal audit function, which can also supply training, but that the operating units and functions must own the process. It also helps if risk assessment is an integral part of the strategic planning process. The three-year Strategic Plan can then be presented to the board by the CEO with the corporate risk assessment. This fulfills the board's annual review requirement. I would also suggest that the corporate risk assessment be updated as part of the development of the annual operating plan which will also be reviewed by the board.

The corporate risk assessment is built from the bottom-up by each operating unit and function with the most critical risks captured as the assessments move up through the corporate levels. So each country would have its risk assessment in its strategic plan even though that country's risks might not have been critical enough to be captured in the region's or corporate risk assessment.

A RISK MATRIX

A risk matrix is a simple tool for facilitating the construction of a risk assessment at each step. The matrix is designed to capture the financial impact and probability for each key risk.

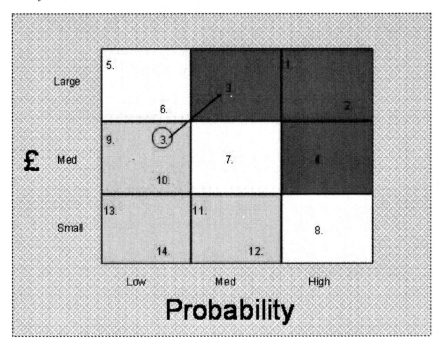

Figure 8.1   A risk matrix.

Arrows within the matrix can also be used to demonstrate how risk items have changed in cost impact or probability since the previous strategic or operating plan. For example, in the illustration, risk #3 has become more probable and costlier since the previous plan.

MITIGATION IS KEY

Risk identification and quantification begin the process, but without proper mitigation, Higgs's call for "robust and effective risk management" will not be achieved. For each risk identified and quantified at each level of a corporation, there must be a mitigation action or series of actions, a timetable for achievement of each mitigation step and identification of the executive responsible. At the corporate level, the person responsible would be one of the CEO's executive team or, in some cases, the CEO. Mitigation actions that merely call for study or review should be discouraged. Study should move on to implementation of true mitigation measures.

WILL THIS RISK MODEL HELP TO SUSTAIN PROFITABILITY?

It might if the board encourages an open and an honest risk assessment process. The CEO of one UK bank fired the risk assessment officer who raised serious red flags. The officer was found to be "quirky" and not a "team player." When risks are running rampant because of the operational team, the last thing one should want is for the risk assessment officer to join the team.

Higgs had another key suggestion for "good practice": "Is the composition of the Board and its committees appropriate, with the right mix of knowledge and skills to maximize performance in the light of future strategy? Are inside and outside the board relationships working effectively?" Sadly, the answer in too many cases should have been NO!

The UK Combined Code is a compendium of excellent principles, sound requirements and suggestions for good practice. It takes strong and independent boards to ensure authentic compliance to the requirements of the Code. Without such boards, profit sustainability will be illusory.

REFERENCE

Keenan, J. (2004), Corporate governance in UK/USA boardrooms. *Corporate Governance International Review*, 12, 172–6.

NOTE

1. The Cadbury Report (1992), The Greenbury Report (1995), The Hampel Report (1998), The Higgs Review (2003), The Smith Report (2003).

9   Doing Good Is Good Business

David Roth

SUSTAINABILITY IS THE NEW DISPOSABILITY

For almost 65 years, since the end of World War II, disposability and its twin, planned obsolescence, drove an optimistic consumerism best symbolized by the aggrandizing automobile fins of the American gas guzzlers of the 1950s.

Today, perhaps as another symbol of our times, the auto companies are running on empty. And the ad agencies that encouraged our love affair with the car, self-defrosting refrigerators, and every other modern convenience with a limited warranty are the subject of ironic ridicule in the hit TV drama *Mad Men*.

Marketers world over are sill in the business of divining our motivations for profit but their probes of the human psyche reveal a significant shift in attitude about the amount of money we expect to spend and on what we are prepared to spend it.

The rules of commercial engagement have changed. We humans still are acquisitive animals, desire nice things, and remain fundamentally self-interested. However, we feel that our personal resources are limited. And we have begun to recognize that the Earth's resources are limited as well. While self-interest remains our primal motivator, we understand that, on this crowded planet, our self-interest often is best served by working in a cooperative rather than adversarial manner.

The old metaphors no longer work. The seller is not a hunter attempting to ensnare the buyer. Increasingly, buyer and seller form a paired unit seeking products that will serve the former and provide profit to the latter without harming the Earth's climate or any of its peoples.

All marketers, suppliers and retailers will feel the impact of this change, which is more than a transient response to the difficult economy. Rather, we are witnessing a permanent shift in purchasing behavior and the nature of consumption. Market leaders are embracing this change by embedding social and communal values into their business propositions.

For these companies, Corporate Social Responsibility (CSR) is not an add-on. It is not a palliative to absolve the corporation for the sins against the environment, nor is it simply a tactic for ingratiating the corporation to its customers. It is fundamental criterion that will be important for defining business success.

While it remains axiomatic that a successful business needs to be profitable and reward all of its stakeholders, the public will not regard a business as successful unless it achieves its results ethically and with scrupulous regard for the Earth and its inhabitants. The new metric of success asks not only if you made a profit but also how you made a profit.

The consequences are real. All things being equal, shoppers will spend their money with businesses that share their values and punish those that do not.

NOT JUST PHILANTHROPY

Both corporate social responsibility and corporate philanthropy impact positively on the health and welfare of society. Both serve important but different functions.

Corporate philanthropy is about how a corporation spends a small proportion of its profits. A corporate philanthropic gift is a limited transaction between the giver and the recipient. Both recipient and giver receive a dividend. The recipient increases resources for curing disease, providing educational opportunities or broadening the audience for cultural events. For the giver, philanthropy pays a dividend in the form of enhanced prestige.

CSR is about how a business earns all of its profits. It is more than transactional; it is cultural. Because CSR is a way of doing business that is infused throughout an organization, it broadly impacts the many constituencies within, affiliated with and touched by the organization. CSR can motivate and inspire the loyalty of staff, customers, suppliers and shareholders.

In this sense, CSR can produce positive long-term results, perhaps far greater than those achieved by philanthropy alone. But CSR can be more complicated to implement especially when it relates to sustainability and requires cooperation at every link in the supply chain.

DOING GOOD IS GOOD BUSINESS

Supply chains are complicated. Being responsible about the products we offer and offering them at a good price is not always easy. Purchasing decisions can have unforeseen and unintended consequences. But, as the following examples illustrate, it is possible to be both responsible and profitable.

B&Q

In the mid-1990s, home improvement centers in Europe were doing big business in garden furniture sourced from Southeast Asia. The suppliers and retailers made money. Consumers got a good price. Everyone was obliviously happy until an enterprising journalist asked B&Q, the largest home center in the UK, where it sourced its wood.

When the then marketing director, Bill Whiting, answered that he did not know, the journalist responded: Don't know means don't care. Whiting could not get the exchange out of his head. And he soon discovered two troubling facts. First, that some garden furniture wood was harvested from endangered forests. Second, no mechanism existed for verifying the provenance of wood from these remote forests.

With a group of partners, B&Q engaged the entire supply chain, from forest to retail, and supported tracking and traceability systems to ensure that the wood for garden furniture was responsibly harvested. Within a few years, most of the wood was certified as sustainable by the Forest Stewardship Council (FSC).

At the same time, B&Q cultivated consumer awareness of how products bought for backyard comfort in Europe impact tropical forests in developing regions of the world. B&Q's leadership proved good for the endangered forests, for the climate that forests help stabilize and for sales.

Walmart

Walmart provides an important example of CSR and concern for sustainability because its environmental commitment is a core business strategy and, as the world's largest retailer, its impact is enormous.

Walmart established an Environmental Advisory Board in 1989. In 1993, the company opened an experimental "green" store, in Lawrence, Kansas, which emphasized energy-efficient technologies and materials in the store's construction and operations.

The company slowly expanded its environmental program during the 1990s and through the early years of this century. Meanwhile, the chain came under intense scrutiny for its impact on the environment and its labour practices.

Initially defensive, Walmart ultimately collaborated with some of its critics, including NGOs. The company's conciliatory and proactive approach helped repair its reputation for corporate good citizenship, which it deemed important for maintaining relationships with long-time customers and for expanding its base of more urban and affluent customers. The company's initiatives include:

- *Product Range*: In 2007, Walmart pledged to sell 100 million energy-efficient compact fluorescent light bulbs within one year—and it met that goal.
- *Sustainability Index*: In July 2009, Walmart announced that it would create a sustainability index that it will apply to all of its products, an effort that is likely to affect is roughly 100,000 vendors.

- *Project Impact*: In another far-reaching initiative, Walmart has launched a remodeling program aimed at reducing the size of its stores and the amount of merchandise and packaging they contain.

Equally important, Walmart's environmental initiatives are linked to the "virtuous circle" that has been at heart of the corporate strategy since Sam Walton opened his first store. Environmentally related efficiencies—such as recycling, eliminating packaging, and improving fleet management—produce cost reductions that enable the lower prices that drive sales volume.

As H. Lee Scott, Jr., told an audience at the National Retail Federation convention, in New York, in January 2009, in one of his last speeches as Walmart CEO:

> There is no conflict between delivering value to shareholders and helping to solve bigger societal problems. In fact, they can build on each other when developed executed and aligned properly.
>
> At Walmart we do not see it as philanthropy or CSR or the triple bottom line. We believe you can bring together the bottom line and the balance sheet with the societal and environmental bottom lines.

Proctor & Gamble

Proctor & Gamble claims that about three billion people, or half of the Earth's inhabitants, are consumers of its household and personal care products.

To understand the needs of such a broad consumer base, the company has made diversity a business strategy that, when linked with collaboration, becomes a competitive advantage.

"We may be messier getting started, may need to work harder to figure out how to work across cultures and languages," said P&G chairman A. G. Lafley. "But we're going to come up with more ideas and create something that will make a difference."

Because P&G views itself as a company that creates products, from laundry detergent to skin care, that primarily are bought and consumed by women, the company is especially engaged with women's health issues.

"I've become a huge believer in that the health of an economy relies on the health of women in an economy," said Lafley. "Do they get an education? Do they have birth control information? Do they have access to medical practitioners? What's the health of their babies at birth?"

The company conducts educational programs for girls' hygiene and operates mobile and in-school dental facilities for children in various parts of the world. It runs a safe drinking water program and has built schools in China.

B&Q, Walmart, and P&G, two retailers and a supplier, are examples of companies that operate successful internationally businesses, which impact the Earth and its inhabitants. The companies share another important characteristic: each is informed by an ethic which asserts that doing good is good business.

BEST PRACTICES

The key point is not that these companies operate perfectly, but that they are earnest in their commitment to corporate social responsibility. And they are not alone.

Among enlightened businesses, this concern with corporate social responsibility touches a broad range of issues including responsible sourcing, employee welfare and poverty in the developing world. Concern with CSR was perhaps jolted and accelerated by the urgent need to slow the negative impact that business has had on the Earth's climate.

Since the advent of industrialization, in the mid-1700s, the concentration of carbon dioxide in the Earth's atmosphere has increased by about 30%. Without remediation, climate change could become irreversible in only two decades.

Governments have a role in this remediation as they did during the early years of industrialization, in the 19th century, by enacting laws to prohibit child labour and regulate other abuses. Today, however, the agents of remediation include NGOs and businesses as well as governments.

The many reasons why entities other than government are engaged in these problems include globalization—the sense that we are all interconnected citizens of the planet and communication—the ability to immediately and constantly exchange information that reinforces our connectedness. The engagement of business involves other reasons:

- Customers prefer to do businesses with organizations that they trust, a trust that was sorely tested by the global financial crisis.
- Employees prefer to work with organizations that they can feel proud of, that do not harm others or damage the Earth.
- Shareholders prefer to invest in companies that produce strong returns while acting as good corporate citizens.

Here are some suggested best practices for CSR, particularly as it relates to product sourcing and sustainability:

Transparency: Provide consumers with all the information necessary to make purchasing decisions. Along with the normal descriptions of a product's performance and efficacy, customers increasingly want to understand the social and environmental impact of the products they use. Be honest. Consumers forgive imperfection but punish deceit.

Responsible Innovation: It may be innovative to create MP3 players and other products with just enough style and color change to prompt annual disposal and repurchase. But it is also irresponsibly wasteful. Many consumers now reject excess; even more can no longer afford it. Most will welcome real innovation but lose patience and respect for changes simply calculated to rip notes from their wallets. Purchases will be more considered and practical. Products, like the most enduring examples of civilization, will be valued for their timelessness.

Differentiation: A sincere commitment to sustainability will win customer respect and purchases. And it will differentiate a company from its competition. The key word is "sincere." "Greenwashing," a veneer of concern coating business as usual, is easy to see through and dismiss. The resulting brand damage can be fatal.

Integrity: People do not feel comfortable compartmentalizing their lives. They expect the same standards of decency and ethical behavior to apply whether they are working, shopping or spending time with family and friends. Businesses that depart from this consistency create dissonance and risk losing customers.

Talking Points: If you're not sure whether your products measure up to CSR and sustainability standards, ask them. Imagine your products can talk. What would they say about how their raw materials were provided? How would they describe the conditions in the factories where they were fabricated? Could the products freely share their stories with your customers or, to avoid embarrassment, would you first need to coach them?

All businesses can benefit from integrating a commitment to corporate social responsibility and sustainability into the life of the organization. The marketing community, having been complicit in fostering overconsumption, perhaps has a special responsibility for adopting and advancing CSR and the notion of sustainable consumption.

The marketing community made a lot of money convincing people that they needed to purchase a new car every couple of years or that last fall's fashion was just too last fall. Having contributed to the problem, marketers can help solve it by redirecting their creative power to encourage a more realistic and responsible attitude toward consumption and stewardship of the Earth.

This initiative would be good, and it would be good business.

10 Demonstrating Goodness

Michael Littlechild

There has been a fairly broad consensus in the corporate world for some time that it makes sound business sense to behave oneself. Some businesses bought in sooner than others to the notion that high ethical conduct is part of the process of making money, rather than a mere adjunct or even a complete distraction. Today there are few corporate websites which spare their readers a lecture on the company's ethical credentials. The terminology can vary—ethics, sustainability, corporate responsibility (social or otherwise)—but they are all essentially variations on the same theme.

At the same time most companies are only too aware that they are facing a skeptical audience. Our trust that companies do what they say has not significantly shifted since the days when businesses were silent about their ethics and hoped we would either not find out or care. Edelman still finds that only 38% of British citizens ('informed public') trust companies to do what is right, a little behind their trust in governments (44%), but well ahead of faith in media (28%), ironically the source of most of our information on the misdemeanors of business (July 2009 survey). These results are roughly the same for many Continental European countries, although these tend to be less cynical about the media. Americans on the other hand have a history of trusting companies much more than Europeans. The crisis of capitalism of the past two years, and the role of banks especially, caused their faith in companies to nosedive in 2009, with a 20% drop in trust to the same levels we are used to in Europe, only to bounce back to long-run levels in 2010.

So what have businesses been doing to convince a doubting public? A whole bundle of activities have been tried, abandoned, rehashed and retried, and still we seem to remain unconvinced. I have divided these efforts to impress into four main categories.

RE-BRANDING

A number of sectors have been at the forefront of using corporate image and communications to persuade us of their ethics. This is not just regular public relations but an attempt to redefine the very identity of the company. Oil and gas and retail are sectors where this has been very evident. BP discarded the British Petroleum identity long ago, somewhat later redefining itself as Beyond Petroleum. This came complete with a green flower logo and matching prime-time advertising, in which the focus was more on harmony with the natural environment than the more muscular imagery of drilling holes and flaring gas. Sainsbury's reassured us that they were the first supermarket to stop selling caged eggs, that they source ethically from farmers and that their carrier bags are reusable. These companies are quite typical of their sectors nowadays, the main differentiator being which caught on to it sooner rather than later. Essentially, however, this re-branding exercise has been, at best, an attempt to persuade us through positioning rather than to provide us with any real evidence that there is reality behind the message.

CLUBBING

An approach which goes back to the dawn of time for Corporate Social Responsibility (CSR)—some 20 odd years ago—is to associate with other like-minded companies to proclaim the importance of good corporate conduct and to strive together for improvement. Business in the Community in the UK was a pioneer in this field, born of an era when serious social disorder in deprived inner cities led companies to reflect upon the role they could have in bringing long-term solutions to such problems. Since then, fraternal bodies have set up in most Western economies as well as further afield.

These clubs are mostly open to all comers. There are no entry qualifications or minimum ethical tests to pass before you can rub shoulders with the leading exponents of CSR. The spirit is that anyone can join, ethical warts and all, and learn from others how things can be done better. Membership is therefore no great measure of good conduct, though some associations do create league tables of their members. There is no doubt however that many companies join in the hope of benefiting from "innocence by association." Certainly most are quick to tell us of their membership and, where they can, their high rankings in the performance tables.

CERTIFYING AND INDEXING

An obvious further step is to obtain third-party endorsement through certification or by qualifying for ethical stock exchange indexes which set and evaluate entry criteria.

Certification for ethical purposes is an extension of certification for quality, which has been a success in setting standards for a whole variety of products and services. The closest standard of relevance to ethics is ISO

14001 on environmental management. This is universally regarded as a model for good environmental practice, though some of the faith put in it is based on a misunderstanding of what it stands for. ISO 14001 focuses on environmental management systems, with formalized processes for measuring impacts and defining and following up remedial actions. It does not insist on any particular limits for emissions or rate of improvement for their reduction. Attempts to reproduce a similar approach to certifying CSR, a behavioural concept which cannot be easily and universally defined, have had to change course and ISO has provided guidelines for social responsibility (ISO 26000) rather than a certified standard.

Ethical stock exchange indexes are subsets of listed companies which qualify as good or sustainable, the leaders being FTSE4Good and the Dow Jones Sustainability Index. They are directed toward the market for socially responsible investment, though this represents such a small proportion of investment funds that they are unlikely to have any material effect on the flow of funds to good companies' stocks. For most companies the importance of membership is at least as much as a badge of respectability, again shown by the prominent position that membership is given in company communications.

The ethical indexes have developed over time, and their selection criteria have become more sophisticated and demanding. There is no doubt that they have been part of the forces of change persuading companies to take ethics seriously. However, the selection criteria still need to be based on fairly simple, document-based evidence of ethics, which is traceable and visibly impartial. Inevitably they cannot go very deeply into testing how far policies are followed in reality. They also have not shown that ethics as judged by them have a strong performance advantage. The FTSE4Good index has historically fluctuated very closely in line with the All World index, though disappointingly at a lower level.

PUBLIC REPORTING

The most direct attempt to demonstrate the sincerity of corporate ethical claims is the practice of public reporting. Serving as a companion to the Annual Report and Accounts, this report (variously named "social," "sustainability" or some combination) sets out to present objectively the non-financial performance of the company and is targeted at the company's stakeholders rather than shareholders. Such reports have become very common coinage. According to a survey by KPMG in 2008, some 85 of the UK's top 100 companies produced stand-alone reports. This was second only to Japan with 88, while in the United States, late arrivals on the ethical reporting stage, it was 72, over double the number in 2005.

The reports have a broadly common coverage, typically consisting of stakeholder sections, but they vary enormously in length, style and the extent to which they serve to promote a positive image rather than genuinely report on the company's strengths and weaknesses. They all contain significant amounts of data, with many following the Global Reporting Initiative (GRI), a UN-sponsored framework which harmonizes the data to be included in such reports and how it should be defined and expressed.

Many of the reporters also have aspects of the reports verified by independent companies to ensure the reader that the content is well founded. For the serious reporters the whole exercise involves a significant commitment of internal resource as well as expenditure on verification and communications. Because of the need for verifiers to validate a defined text, most reports are still produced annually in hard copy, though all are available online and many companies also have web-based, continuously updated reporting.

Given all these sterling efforts, what can have gone wrong to cause us to persist in distrusting corporate sincerity? I would underline two main problems. The first relates to business behavior itself, namely the slow progress made toward embedding corporate responsibility into the everyday activities of the business, beyond specific CSR activities. The second relates to the reporting of ethical performance, with inherent flaws in the approach both to coverage and verification.

GAPS BETWEEN THEORY AND PRACTICE

The most important factor undermining confidence is the public demonstration that businesses have fallen short of their ethical pledges. Many illustrations appear in our newspapers on a daily basis.

In 2005 the Group Chief Executive of Barclays was saddened to discover that the Daily Telegraph believed that banking was behind as a sector in CSR. "It was clear to me," he said in his corporate responsibility statement, "that, despite our efforts in the past, we still had a lot to do to convince our stakeholders that we are absolutely serious about corporate responsibility. The best way I can do this is to say that everything we do under the 'corporate responsibility' banner is directly relevant to our business goals." In 2007, however, by which time one might have expected corporate responsibility to have reached even higher levels, an undercover BBC reporter produced a powerful television report showing Barclays staff being trained to be anything but responsible, indeed to sell products inappropriately to customers. We watched as a call-center trainer explained to trainees how he loved getting customers complaining about bank charges. "I was thinking 'you are not getting it back'. I was a right git."

Balfour Beatty in 2006 was a leading light in CSR in the UK construction sector, a member of the Dow Jones Sustainability Index and the outright winner of Construction News' Corporate Responsibility Award. At the same time, as was discovered two years later by the Office of Fair Trading, the company was one of 40 businesses in the industry colluding over bidding for public contracts, resulting in clients such as local authorities overpaying.

BP's Sustainability Report of 2004 highlighted pipeline integrity as a key element in its management of environmental risk. However, in 2006 in two separate incidents some 5000 barrels of oil were leaked onto the Alaskan tundra, which led to investigations by a Federal Grand Jury as well as both the Houses of Congress. They all criticized BP in the United States not just for technical failure but for management neglect, resulting in BP having to commit to a series of major management and operational changes. Included in the solution was the appointment of a U.S. District Court judge to act as an independent ombudsperson for BP's U.S. employees to ensure that their concerns about these or any other operational issues would be investigated and resolved. The conclusion that the company had to accept was that management had ignored employees' concerns. Similar conclusions had been reached by investigators of two fires the year before at BP's Texas City Refinery, which resulted in fatalities. The damage to BP's reputation in North America continued right up to April 2010, when the Gulf of Mexico catastrophe caused reputational damage to the company on an uprecendented scale.

How could these things happen in such large, sophisticated companies? Why would leading businessmen risk such public embarrassment, not to say exposure in the courts? Were the CSR claims they made always intended to be a big bluff? Did those chief executives think we were all naïve, or maybe just a bit thick? Or did they perhaps not know what was going on in their own companies? None of these explanations makes pleasant reading for their employees and customers, or their shareholders for that matter. I am inclined to favor a different explanation, relating to their limited vision of CSR. I strongly suspect that they had such things as customer mis-selling, collusion with competitors, and poor safety and engineering integrity in a completely different box. Despite the all-embracing statement of the bank, I think these companies' senior executives still had CSR pigeon-holed with community projects, employee diversity and tree planting. Odd though it may seem to the layman, they simply did not have honest selling, fair competition and environmental risk management in their dictionary definition of corporate responsibility.

FLAWS IN REPORTING

If there are gaps between codes of conduct and actual practice, the process of reporting on practice also has some significant flaws. The content of many CSR reports still has a strong promotional feel. It is true that some companies have gone further in baring their souls and admitting their own mistakes, though in many cases this is because the story is already out and it would not be credible to do much else. The reports also contain a lot of data, which one would hope could not lie. However, at close inspection much of the data given constitutes long rambling lists of numbers that reveal little or nothing without corresponding context or benchmarks. Rarely are we given ready-made time series which could at least help identify trends. The GRI has gone a long way to standardize definitions of data and increase the demand for statistics but that has often exacerbated rather than reduced the problem of numbers for numbers' sake. So by following its requirements, a multinational can inform the public that the number of cases of alleged competition infringements under judicial review is six, the number of supplier audits performed is 23 and the number of community initiatives is 46. When one reads these long lists of data, one is continuously struck that a crucial test has not been passed, or more likely not even been applied, namely: are these numbers interesting or meaningful for any stakeholder?

Even if some of this data is relevant to stakeholders' interest, it is often not clear how to interpret good results from bad. If customer complaints have fallen, this is presumably good news. Unless of course the company has made it harder in some way to complain or its poor response to earlier complaints has discouraged customers from bothering to do so (which, as all of us know, happens too often). Similar question marks are attached to health and safety statistics, which tend to worsen as companies improve their reporting mechanisms.

Further flaws in current reporting approaches lie in the limitations of the external verification process. It is a common misconception that a verified report has somehow been completely validated for its content, whereas in fact the extent of independent verification is generally very limited. A typical assurance statement, contained at the back of a report of a major international company with a long-standing reporting history, illustrates the point:

> *Level of assurance:* Our evidence gathering procedures have been designed to obtain a limited level of assurance (as set out in ISAE 3000) on which to base our conclusions. The extent of evidence gathering procedures performed is less than that of a reasonable assurance engagement (such as a financial audit) and therefore a lower level of assurance is provided.

> *The limitations of our review:* The scope of our work was limited to group level activities. We did not visit any of the company's businesses. Our stakeholder engagement activities were limited to attendance at one event. Therefore, our conclusions on Materiality and Responsiveness are based on our discussions with the company's management, our review of selected media and the review of documents provided to us by the company.

On the face of it, it is hardly a testimony to exhaustive rigor. Other statements in a lengthy text use language abounding in double negatives. "Nothing has come to our attention that causes us to believe that HSE, community investment and ethics dismissals data has not been properly collated." Auditors are naturally keen to ensure that they primarily check data which can be practically validated, to protect their own reputations and manage their risk. As a result, even within the constraints of these strong caveats, the validation is focused essentially on whether statistical data is accurate rather than whether it means much, let alone how well company policies are adhered to in reality.

DO BETTER OR GIVE UP

Is this a hopeless situation? Are companies doomed to be disbelieved about their ethical sincerity because everyone believes that they are just out to make money, come what may? I think there are some straightforward but significant ways in which things can be done a lot better and they will save, not cost money.

1. Don't do Annual Social Reports

Annual reports, hard copy or web only, are old hat and not worth the yearly crescendo of internal activity. Needing a fixed text on which auditors can pin their verification is no good reason to annualize the report, given the limitations of the validation exercise. A flow of updated information does better.

2. Report on how Business is Done, not just the Trimmings

Corporate responsibility and ethics are empty concepts if they are not about how a company does business—how it treats the people who work for it, the customers who buy from it, the suppliers that sell to it, the other organizations and people that surround it and are affected by it, as well as the rest of the planet. This may seem a huge truism, but it still seems lost on many of those who run businesses. The largesse handed out to worthy causes in money and kind is interesting but, as it accounts for less than 1% of profits in even the most generous companies, it is worth a few paragraphs. Besides, being generous is not the same as being ethical.

3. Get Independent Verification of how You do Business, not of what You Write About it

A code of ethics needs to be clear about what real business practices a company uses, not just what generic values it expounds. There is no point in claiming it supports the local supply chain if it pays its suppliers late, or that it believes in customer transparency if it plays tricks with pricing extras on its website, or that it is striving to reduce its environmental footprint when it is really just ensuring it does not exceed legal limits and is not fined. It is worth verifying these things and telling stakeholders the results.

4. Report Stakeholder Feedback Openly

Some businesses are leading the way in not just listening to stakeholders but publishing the dialogue. This fits well with continuously updated web reporting and shows a serious intent in dealing with comments and challenges to integrity and ethics. It does though require a different mindset from the orthodox one of "managed" external communications. But then we have seen how little attention people pay to that.

5. End the Avalanche of Meaningless Numbers

Reporting standards and initiatives have created a mystique about CSR data which is undeserved. Data needs to be of interest and meaningful to one stakeholder or another to justify the sweat of collection and publication. Applying this test will cut down the volume we get but should ensure that it is information rather than numbers.

6. Be Modest

It is better to be realistic about ethical claims than to confuse long-term aspiration for current reality. If the company has started on something which is work in progress, it is a mistake to present it as a tried and tested value. Many a company is still hurting from getting this wrong in the distant past. Every company should make a point of asking itself the question posed earlier regarding whether their sincerity is credible. If it concludes that disbelief really is a given, then it is an important conclusion to reach, so that the whole CSR and communications charabanc can pack up its kit and move off.

11 Sustainable Special Economic Zones
A Call to Action

Richard Broyd, Jeff Grogan, Alexandra Mandelbaum, Alejandro Gutierrez and Debra Lam

EXECUTIVE SUMMARY

The World Bank has defined 2301 special economic zones (SEZs) in 119 countries, which account for approximately US $200 billion in gross exports per year. The current economic and environmental crises present a unique window of opportunity to highlight a new development model which focuses on efforts to simultaneously achieve economic and environmental sustainability. Such a strategy can be highly differentiating and enhance the SEZs' chance for longer-term success.

To achieve economic sustainability an SEZ should, through specialization and cluster-based economic strategy, support regional efforts to boost entrepreneurialism, innovation and productivity. To achieve environmental sustainability, an SEZ must work to reduce its own ecological footprint and that of its supply chains.

There are a number of steps that an SEZ can take to pursue the transformation toward economic and environmental sustainability. These include:

- *Conduct an economic and environmental strategic audit.* An SEZ should assess its assets, capabilities, and challenges across four key impact areas: governance and policy, economic competitiveness, carbon footprint, and infrastructure and spatial planning. The SEZ should assess the governance framework, economic performance and the business environment of the region in which it operates, identify the key stakeholders and the composition of industry clusters, and assess the climate for entrepreneurship and regulatory policy. The SEZ should understand its unique role in contributing to the competitiveness of the region. In turn, the SEZ should also identify ways to reduce its carbon footprint by co-locating elements clustering manufacturers and emphasizing clean, green manufacturing practices and strong spatial planning, built around industrial ecology, circular economy, and cyclical industry cluster concepts.
- *Develop economic and environmental goals and a corresponding strategic plan.* Informed by the results of the economic and environmental

strategic audit, the SEZ should develop a strategy defining the actions required to create economic and environmental sustainability.

- *Identify and ensure alignment among key stakeholders.* To successfully enact change, an SEZ should leverage existing institutions and formalize new processes as necessary to ensure cross-collaboration among key stakeholders in an effort to create consensus and alignment behind the strategy.
- *Monitor and report progress.* Finally, SEZ leadership should identify and monitor a set of relevant metrics, identify areas of success and shortcomings relative to the strategic plan, and provide the appropriate actions to address those shortcomings. The metrics should support and complement the governance and policy framework.

INTRODUCTION

Since the 1950s, special economic zones (SEZs) have proliferated as a way to attract businesses and investors by promising investment incentives, and liberal rules and regulations.

Unfortunately, the rules and regulations have rarely addressed curtailing waste production or included incentives for companies and individuals to consider their ecological impact. The more rules and regulations an SEZ applies, the argument goes, the more likely it will lose business to other less-stringent competitors. As such, a "race to the bottom" takes shape whereby SEZs compete to have the leanest environmental standards or the most lax enforcement and monitoring measures in place in order to attract business and investment.

A consensus has emerged that the "old" model of "industrialize, get dirty, get rich, clean up later" is both unwise and unnecessary. The current economic and environmental crises present a unique window of opportunity to highlight a new development model. Such a "new" model focuses instead on efforts to simultaneously achieve economic and environmental sustainability.[2]

Believing that environmental and economic goals are not mutually exclusive, Arup and Monitor Group have collaborated to contribute our ideas on how emerging economies including China, Korea and India might continue to build their economic competitiveness while working to meet their carbon reduction targets. There have already been some positive developments in this direction.[3]

In the pages that follow, we describe how sustainable special economic zones (SSEZs) can serve as a vehicle to do this. We define SSEZs as special economic zones which, through their composition and operational practices, not only build the competitiveness of the region in which they reside but also test and demonstrate environmentally sustainable infrastructure and practices which can then be rolled out to other SEZs, and other regions. For example, in China, we see SEEZs as one opportunity

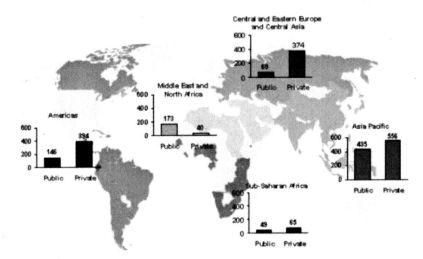

Figure 11.1 Distribution of private sector and public sector zones in developing and transition economies.
Note: zones exclude single factory programs; Countries on the map are indicative and not exhaustive.
Source: Special Economic Zones Performance, Lessons Learned, and implications for Zone Development, Foreign Investment Advisory Services, April 2008[1]

to provide leadership on addressing the post-Kyoto carbon arrangements and to continue their Circular Economy policies against growing economic pressures. But there are more opportunities applicable to other places all over the world, as the principles of economic and environmental sustainability are universal.

While the ideas presented here can apply to SEZs currently being developed, our focus is on the thousands of SEZs already in place; SEZs which now struggle to grow economically and produce substantial amounts of carbon dioxide, air and water pollutants, and waste.

The ideas that follow are directed at SEZ administrators, government officials, and business leaders alike. The current economic and environmental challenges present important opportunities for these individuals to explore new paths toward progress. Our intention is for these ideas to meaningfully contribute to current thinking on economic and environmental sustainability, and we hope that the described way forward guides these leaders and decision makers to successfully implement the ideas.

THE CASE FOR ECONOMIC AND ENVIRONMENTAL SUSTAINABILITY

An economic goal of any nation or region is a high and rising standard of living. This depends upon creating a business environment that fosters entrepreneurialism, innovation and rising productivity. Strong, competitive *clusters* of industry are an important component of this business environment.[4,5]

Being *economically sustainable* means that a region has created a business environment which not only supports a number of competitive clusters in the region but also provides the opportunity for new clusters to emerge, grow and flourish.

Environmental sustainability refers to taking steps to: lower the region's carbon footprint; efficiently produce and consume energy; adequately manage waste; install energy-efficient infrastructure; improve spatial planning and design to emphasize mixed land use patterns, residential and employment density; and provide accessible and efficient public transport, quality open spaces that enhance biodiversity and a circular economy for material resource flows.

Regretfully, the history of economic growth parallels the history of environmental decline. Economic growth has typically occurred in devastatingly direct proportion to increased energy consumption, production waste, carbon emissions, and other actions harmful to the environment. Many who focus on environmental sustainability believe that it cannot be coupled with any type of fast-paced economic growth. In some of the world's fastest growing economies such as China, India, Brazil and Russia, economic expansion has come largely with the price of environmental degradation.

Other nations seen as at the forefront of environmental sustainability such as Finland, Norway, and Sweden have well-developed economies and are now seen as able to "afford" environmentally sustainable development efforts, though environmental damage was incurred at an earlier stage of their industrialization history.

As climate change becomes a defining issue of the 21st century, capturing the public and media's attention, prompting wide-ranging political discussion on an improved international climate action plan, and driving new business strategies, the concept of environment and economic mutual exclusivity is being challenged. Such plans and strategies recognize that the growing inefficiencies and waste generation results not only in environmental degradation, but also diminished economic competitiveness. By moving to more environmentally sustainable economic growth, a virtuous cycle forms where people, even in developing economies, begin to demand environmental sustainability. Environmental sustainability becomes an integral part of economic sustainability.

SEZS AS DEMONSTRATION ZONES
FOR SUSTAINABLE DEVELOPMENT

Special economic zones afford a unique opportunity to demonstrate how economic and environmental sustainability can work in tandem. Today, most SEZs have had difficulty differentiating themselves from one another. However, a strategy built on both economic and environmental sustainability can be highly differentiating and can enhance the SEZs chance for longer-term success. There are examples of SEZs that have set targets for environmental sustainability, in China, India and the Middle East.

As the region enhances its economic competitiveness, it will have a growing cadre of people focused on environmental sustainability. SEZ stakeholders can lead the way and collaborate to improve the environmental impact of SEZs, while enhancing and marketing their economic success.[6]

SEZs have formed for a variety of reasons. Some have been formed as "pressure valves" to avoid more difficult structural reform in the immediate term or, as a catalyst for reform, allowing the nation to pilot and test new programs and approaches before implementing them nationally. In other regions SEZs have been created to attract investment and stimulate economic growth.

Many SEZs have traditionally competed on price and tax rebates in order to attract businesses and workers. Many have failed to focus on the local strengths of a region and have failed to create the conditions upon which they can successfully compete. Their economic strategies have been neither differentiated nor value-driven. Focused on manufacturing and industrial sectors, many have failed to attract knowledge-based industries, the technological know-how and the talent necessary to become a center of innovation. Many SEZs have failed to attract foreign investors, provide meaningful levels of employment, or support cross-border trade and knowledge transfer efforts. These failures have led these SEZs to consider ways to be "de-notified" from SEZ status so that developers might pursue other uses of the real estate.[7, 8]

Environmentally, SEZs conditions have typically been dismal. Companies and industries within SEZs have been frequently governed by liberal environmental regulations that neither curtail waste production nor incentivize companies and individuals to consider their ecological impact. SEZs believe that if they regulate too much, they will lose investment to other less stringently regulated competitors. For industrial companies requiring large physical footprints and producing substantial amounts of waste, strict environmental regulations can, at least in the short term, be the difference between profits and losses. SEZs have competed to have the lowest environmental standards or most lax enforcement and monitoring in order to attract the most business and investment.[9, 10]

Today, the World Bank has defined 2301 SEZs in 119 countries, which account for approximately US $200 billion in gross exports per year. China specifically accounts for around 19% of these zones.

While there have been some success stories as well, varied levels of success among SEZs point to the need for a new model for thinking about long-term economic and environmental sustainability. SEZs particular governance and policy status, distinct from the rest of the region or nation, allows them to serve as laboratories for new legal structures which can be carved out of national legislation for experimental and demonstration purposes. The SEZ, therefore, is an ideal focal point for proving the advantages of a new model at a time when the traditional economic competitiveness metrics or environmental merits alone are insufficient, and the pressure to form a post-Kyoto climate change agreement is strong.

SUSTAINABLE SPECIAL ECONOMIC ZONES

The past failings of SEZs do not have to be their future reality. Governments and industry participants are interested in sensible solutions. Operators realize that effective management of the environment is a key attraction for potential investors. As such, SEZs that focus on developing their economies and nurturing their environments can position themselves for long-term growth.

To achieve economic sustainability, SEZs must create a business environment which supports cluster-based economic strategy and facilitates entrepreneurialism, innovation and increasing levels of productivity. While there may be up-front costs integrating environmental and economic strategy, failing to couple an economically competitive strategy with environmental consciousness will ultimately be far costlier.[11] In fact, lowering an SEZs environmental impact can also have real economic benefits such as reduced energy costs, lower waste, lower healthcare costs, an improved quality of life, increased innovation and higher productivity.

ACTIONS TO BECOME A SUSTAINABLE
SPECIAL ECONOMIC ZONE

There are a number of steps that an SEZ can take to pursue the transformation towards economic and environmental sustainability. These include:

- **Conduct an economic and environmental strategic audit.** An SEZ should assess its assets, capabilities, and challenges across four key impact areas: governance and policy, economic competitiveness, carbon footprint, and infrastructure and spatial planning.
- **Develop economic and environmental goals and a corresponding strategic plan.** Informed by the results of the economic and environmental strategic audit, the SEZ should prepare a focused mission statement and define the actions required for economic and environmental sustainability. This strategic plan should be binding and linked to economic competitiveness metrics and carbon reduction targets, and it should connect to new Clean Development Mechanisms (CDMs) and other carbon policies.

- **Ensure alignment among key stakeholders.** To successfully enact change, it is important to leverage existing institutions and formalize new processes and institutions as necessary to ensure cross-collaboration among stakeholders and to create consensus behind the strategy and alignment in economic competitiveness and environmental sustainability efforts in support of the strategy.
- **Monitor and report progress.** Finally, SEZ leadership should identify and monitor a set of relevant metrics, identify areas of success and shortcomings relative to the strategic plan, and provide the appropriate actions to address those shortcomings. The metrics should support and complement the governance and policy framework.

A description of each of these steps is provided below:

Conduct an Economic and Environmental Strategic Audit

The strategic audit enables an SEZ to "take stock" of where it stands today relative to four impact areas: governance and policy, economic competitiveness, carbon footprint, and infrastructure and spatial planning.

Governance and Policy

Governance, as defined by the United Nations, refers to "the process by which decisions are implemented (or not implemented)." This definition remains purposefully broad to illustrate that governments are one of many actors that can be involved in the process of governance. Other actors may include financial institutions, businesses, investors, and community leaders, among others.[12]

Good governance frequently shares a set of core values[13]:

- Accountability—government must be explicit about what it is incentivizing (via subsidies) and discouraging (via taxes and fines) and remain accountable to those who will be affected by its decisions or actions;
- Responsiveness—institutions and processes try to serve all stakeholders within a reasonable timeframe; and
- Effectiveness and efficiency—government produces results that meet the needs of society while making sustainable use of resources.

Good governance can drive foreign direct investment, encourage efficiencies in economic activity, support and extend rule of law, and establish the foundation for an equitable and inclusive society that seeks to avoid conflicts peacefully, among other things. Policies, in turn, support and implement governance doctrines. In today's SEZs, policies frequently focus on short-term economic drivers to attract businesses, including tax breaks and incentives. Instead, policies should produce long-term gains and encourage high levels of stakeholder engagement.

The governance and policy audit should make explicit the tax and other business incentives and regulatory policies in place to recruit and retain business investment in the SEZ. It should also map the businesses and financial institutions, which comprise the SEZs stakeholder group and the degree to which the SEZ is effectively and efficiently meeting stakeholder needs.

Economic Sustainability

The productivity and innovative capacity of a regional economy benefit from macroeconomic conditions such as sound fiscal policy and effective political decision-making processes. However, these are increasingly pre-conditions, not sources of competitive advantage. Prosperity in a region is actually created by the microeconomic foundations of competitiveness rooted in the sophistication with which individuals, firms, industries and industry clusters based there compete. This is what gives rise to productivity. The sophistication with which firms compete rests heavily on the quality of the regional business environment in which they operate.[14] Achieving economic sustainability begins with an assessment of a region's economic performance and competitive prospects. Analytical steps include the following:

- *Benchmark the economic performance and innovation output of the region.* An audit of an SEZ's economic sustainability begins with a benchmarking of the region's economic performance and innovation output. Key indicators include statistics related to employment (job creation and unemployment rates), population, wages (wage level and wage growth), establishment formation, and innovation output (patents, fast growth firms), among others. These statistics are then compared against national and regional averages as well as against the region's key competitors. This typically includes regions with similar geographic or demographic composition, as well as high-performing regions whose success can be further studied and, perhaps, replicated.
- *Understand the economic composition of the region.* A second step in assessing economic sustainability is understanding the composition of industry in the region in which the SEZ resides, and the role the SEZ plays in contributing, or not, to the region's competitiveness. In our experience, the most successful regions are specialized. For example, in the United States, New Jersey is very strong in pharmaceuticals, and in Europe, London is strong in financial services.

Economic composition describes the unique set of companies and clusters in a region. The objective of this analysis is to assess the relative size, growth, and economic impact of various clusters of an economy. In addition, the economic composition analysis helps identify relative strengths and regional assets within the SEZ and the region that may provide opportunities to drive economic growth.

Figure 11.2 shows the composition of a selected region. The size of employment in a given cluster is represented by the size of the bubble. The share each cluster contributes to the region's employment is represented by the bubble's position on the vertical axis. The change in share of employment is represented by position on the horizontal axis.

Clusters above the horizontal dotted line have more employment than expected for the region. Clusters to the right of the vertical line are gaining employment share in the region relative to the nation. The clusters in or close to the upper right quadrant are generally the most competitive clusters in the region.

- *Assess the business environment.* The third step in our economic sustainability audit is an analysis of the quality of the business environment in which the SEZ resides and how the SEZ contributes or detracts from this business environment.

To understand the specific strengths and challenges of a given business environment, in-depth interviews with local executives should be conducted. In addition to interviews, a cross-regional survey can be very helpful for benchmarking a region's assets. Monitor uses our *Executive Insight Survey*, which asks a standard set of questions about the business

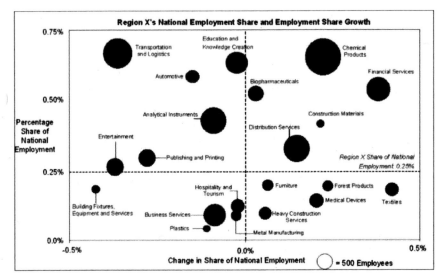

Figure 11.2 The composition of a region's traded industry clusters.

environment, and identifies opportunities to upgrade the business environment by promoting regional strengths and addressing the most pressing issues for local businesses. Topics such as the extent to which there are specialized pools of human resources, technology and infrastructure and capital to support the needs of particular industries; the level of sophistication of customers in a region; the rules, incentives and pressures which govern competition and their influence on productivity; and the presence and strength of related and supporting industries in a region are addressed in this assessment. We follow this survey with in-depth interviews with local executives and government leaders to identify the specific strengths and challenges of the business environment and to identify the most pressing issues and opportunities.

- *Benchmark the competitiveness of key clusters.* In addition to understanding the region as a whole, it is important to examine a select number of the region's industry clusters in more depth. Such an analysis provides a nuanced understanding of how strengths and challenges play-out in different parts of the regional economy. Output from the analysis will not only help the specific cluster in question, but will also inform the overarching regional strategy and how the SEZ might best contribute.

Monitor's approach to cluster prioritization follows a screening process designed to select important regional clusters for further analysis. Filters are used to help identify clusters that offer the optimal mix of economic attractiveness and strategic feasibility. This screening process may include economic performance, innovation and composition metrics as well as other measures of economic impact such as size of addressable market, sociopolitical environment, and competitive position.

We next benchmark the performance of the selected clusters. Through targeted interviews, qualitative research and a focused survey of cluster participants, we map the composition of the cluster and assess the local inputs, competitors, customers and other clusters that impact the cluster's ability to develop, grow and sustain businesses in the given region.

Every cluster is made up of several subclusters, which consist of closely related industries. Subclusters serve to support the overall cluster at various points in its value chain. Figure 11.3 analyzes the flow of products, services, information and ideas through the plastics cluster and provides a broader perspective of the cluster's particular strengths and strengths and weaknesses.

Often, a region that is strong in a cluster is really strong in just a few of its component subclusters. Data-driven cluster maps allow for the identification of relatively stronger and relatively weaker subclusters within clusters in most parts of the world. The stronger the subcluster, the darker the blue is shaded. In general, regions and companies should strive to build broad

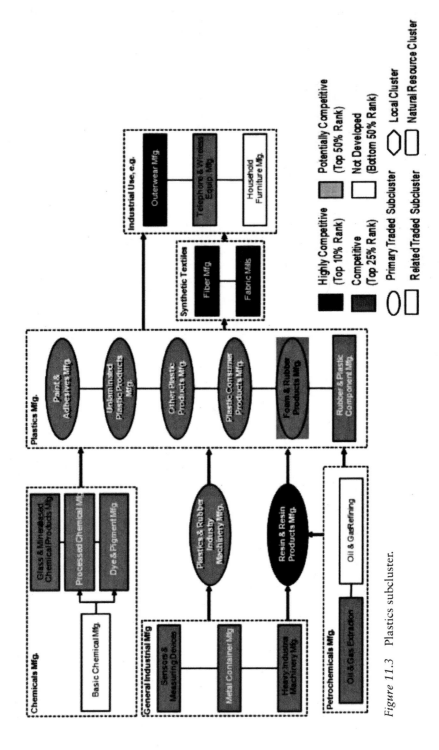

Figure 11.3   Plastics subcluster.

and deep clusters and strength across the numerous subclusters within the cluster. Relatively weaker subclusters indicate areas that a region's marketing and recruiting efforts ought to target.

- *Assess the environment for entrepreneurship.* Few factors have as great an impact in producing innovation, creating jobs, or generally contributing to a dynamic and competitive economy than entrepreneurship. Successful entrepreneurship arises from many factors, including financing, innovative ideas, management skills, and the right set of social, economic, and personal motivations. In any given environment, some of these factors will be available, while others will be lacking. The key challenge for policymakers wishing to promote entrepreneurship is to find which ones are unavailable and how they can be supplied. This, of course, is in itself a complex, entrepreneurial endeavor requiring imagination, will, and negotiation among competing interests. It requires, above all, the ability to identify the binding constraints in the environment so as to develop a feasible plan of action.

Any effective strategy for the promotion of entrepreneurship must begin with an assessment of the strengths and weaknesses in the environment. Perhaps there is a financing gap for start-ups or approval and registration processes are onerous and opaque. Perhaps entrepreneurial skills and values are not being fostered, or entrepreneurs are deprived of advice due to the absence of networks, business associations, and professional service firms willing to work with new companies. There is no way to know in the abstract which measures are most likely to work for a particular environment.[15]

- *Economic performance and sustainability of the SEZ itself.* With the analysis of the region's economic performance, assessment of the business environment and cluster-specific analysis of the composition of industry clusters complete, we can then turn to a similar analysis of the SEZ. Such an analysis would include an audit of the SEZ's assets and resources, the composition of industry and industry clusters within the SEZ, and the relative competitiveness of cluster subcomponents. This analysis would enable us to identify how the SEZ might best contribute to the economic sustainability of the region.

Carbon Footprint

Carbon footprint is an accurate indicator of an area's environmental sustainability. Undertaking a carbon footprint analysis of modern SEZs is likely to highlight the consequences of continual economic growth with little regard to biophysical limits.[16] To prove our theories, the team took an example SEZ in China, and estimated the carbon footprint to be 9.3 tonnes per person. A breakdown of the results can be seen in Figure 11.4.

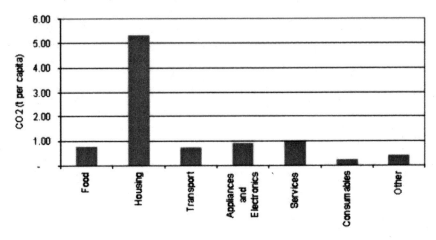

Figure 11.4   Carbon footprint of example Chinese SEZ.

While this is an example SEZ, it is a close reflection of other SEZs around the world, especially in China, and serves our exercise aim of accessing and improving SEZs' economic and environmental sustainability. The footprint is dominated by the energy use in homes. Electricity production makes up 60% of the total carbon footprint of houses, again relating to carbon inefficient electricity production. As a comparison of carbon footprint, Figure 11.5 gives an indication of the footprint of countries across the world, and how an example SEZ compares.

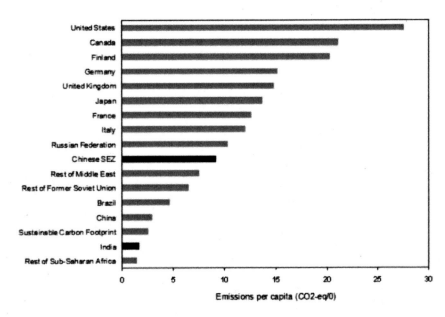

Figure 11.5   Comparative analysis of countries (per capita).

Certainly the comparison does not wholly reflect the different uses and economic activity, and therefore does not define carbon within an SEZ versus the country at large, but it does indicate a baseline scale. The footprint of the residents from the sample SEZ is three times higher than the average person in China, though three times lower than the U.S. resident's footprint. While there is some disagreement on the sustainable carbon footprint, most believe it to be 2.5 tonnes per person.[17] We examined the changing impact over time, to assess whether the SEZ is getting closer or further away from this goal. The trajectory is not encouraging. Since 2003, the carbon footprint of our sample SEZ has grown by 35%, with an average growth rate of 7%/year. To achieve a sustainable carbon footprint by 2050, there needs to be a reduction of 2%/year, mainly through a supply mix of likely renewable and decarbonized energy, accurate estimates of increased grid demands, and supporting infrastructure.

Infrastructure and Spatial Planning

The final impact area that needs to be audited is the infrastructure and spatial planning. This begins with a comprehensive mapping of the building stock, resource flows—transportation, land use and open space, and infrastructure—of the existing site. Using biomimicry principles, the design looks at nature as a model of inspiration; measure for ecological standards to serve as the lasting criteria; and mentor to learn and adapt from.[18] With sufficient understanding and interpretation of the local conditions—economic, social and ecological—and the needs and aspirations of current and future residents, the retrofit master plan for the SSEZ can be grounded on the existing site context.

For transport and access, the current and future transport modes will be detailed, including the carbon shares of each type, fuel options, and transport networks. Transport maps should detail the connections within the SEZs, but also to its regional areas and major cities and waterways. Communications and educational information will be analyzed to see how the public is informed, opined and engaged in their daily and leisure commutes. Goods and service routes and deliveries will also be incorporated into the analysis.

Land use and open space focuses on reducing the demand for motorized travel by enhancing the degree of mix of uses compared to the current mix. Land uses evolve over time, making flexible and temporary land uses important. Land use will incorporate transport, energy, waste and water plans. Studies will be done on the orientation of the prevailing winds, soil conditions, biodiversity, included protected habitats, food production and pollution levels of the different areas. The overall emphasis for the land use and open space will be for a mixed use, high density, biodiverse and integrated community.

Infrastructure addresses resource and waste management and energy and building fabric standards, as well as providing for sustainable energy, water, transport, waste and environmental systems that underpin the sustainable future of the SSEZ and their integration into the wider area. This involves understanding the current consumption levels of waste, water, and energy and the corresponding strategies in dealing with or supplying them to the community. As it is an existing site, the operation, rather than the construction period will be studied.

Equally important will be understanding the existing and future policies and governance operations of the site's infrastructure. Who operates and pays for the waste management? How much does energy cost? What are the government's plans and targets in renewable energy, and does the area have a natural advantage toward a particular type? How do enterprises and consumers use and monitor their water and what kind of education and communications strategy is in place? As each site is different, having this type of information will be critical in producing the specific strategies for the area. Overall though, the principles of minimizing the consumption (or in waste, the production), and supplying it with alternative sources or expanding further uses will be emphasized.

In understanding the infrastructure and spatial planning, it is important to realize the impact on each of the areas—building stock, transport and access; land use and open space; and infrastructure—have on each other, and how their strategies can be leveraged. The waste management can include waste to energy generation, while creating more sustainable transport modes in the land use plans, could lessen the overall infrastructure needs. Analyzing the SEZ's existing infrastructure and spatial features and plans can produce the specialized strategies to transform it into it an SSEZ.

Develop Economic and Environmental Goals and a Corresponding Strategic Plan

Informed by the results of the economic and environmental strategic audit, the SEZ should prepare a set of goals and a strategic plan. The goals and strategic plan detail the specifics of how the SEZ will address the gaps identified in the audit. The process of defining the goals and strategic plan should be viewed as an opportunity to inject into the SEZ's policies new aspirations that will set the stage for long-term sustainability and competitiveness.

An SEZ's goal should be stated simply and at a high level. The goal of an SEZ seeking to become an SSEZ must include the two key components of sustainability: *economic competitiveness* and *environmental impact*. By focusing the goal on the end-result, rather than the process, it can serve as a mission statement to galvanize public support for the SEZ's new direction.

The goal must then be supported with a detailed and action-oriented strategic plan. The strategic plan focuses on the gaps identified from the economic and environmental strategic audit, as well as any additional aspirations that the SEZ wishes to incorporate.

To develop a strategic plan, an SEZ should follow several key steps. These include:

- Prioritizing assets and capabilities it needs to grow or acquire as revealed in the strategic audit. Establishing priorities creates a sequencing of resource investment activity.
- Engaging expert government, economic and environmental leaders who can bring prior experience to bear.
- Considering relevant best practices from other zones, businesses or states in related circumstances.
- Defining specific action items that will address prioritized areas for investment.

Additionally, it is imperative that each of the strategic audit's four impact areas has its own action plans developed during the course of the strategic audit.

An SSEZ will adopt environmentally sustainable practices, and it is likely that there will be opportunities to develop clean technology activities (particularly services) that fill gaps in existing clusters as the SEZ moves toward environmental sustainability. The high environmental standards in SSEZs will also stimulate development of these activities which may, over time, lead to competitive clean technology businesses. However, an SSEZ does not mean an SEZ focused on "clean tech" activities, and is even more unlikely that a clean tech cluster per se will emerge purely on the basis of an SEZ transforming itself into an SSEZ. The team remains skeptical that all the announced stand-alone clean tech clusters are based on differentiated and economically sustainable competitive strategies.

Governance and Policy

Having mapped existing policies, subsequent policies should be primarily focused on longer-term economic and environmental sustainability. This requires developing new policies, refining existing policies—or both—to focus on these goals. Policies are likely to encourage certain actions that may drive long-term investments in the development of human assets, concentration on innovation and idea or technology transfer, and promotion of a higher quality of life, all while recognizing the need to balance a wide portfolio of policy tools and directives.

Each SEZ must identify its own set of appropriate policies that allow it to drive toward the goal of becoming more economically competitive and environmentally sustainable. These policies—supported, enforced and refined through governance—create the foundation on which an SEZ can begin the process of becoming an SSEZ.

Economic Sustainability

A competitive differentiation strategy is necessary for sustainable growth; an SEZ is merely a mechanism. SEZs must be designed as mechanisms to address issues in the business environment that can support and foster the development of clusters which have been identified as part of competitive strategy. Indeed, an SEZ will only address certain aspects of the broader business environment that will be identified as necessary to support the clusters. Where SEZs have been applied as a panacea in and of themselves, it will be luck if they "work." Other important dimensions of the business environment that are beyond the scope of this paper, but critical, include availability of capital and trade policy.

One of the most important ways in which an SEZ can enhance its sustainability is by targeting subcluster growth. No cluster is ever fully complete. Even a very strong regional cluster will have some areas of weakness; it will have some subclusters of buyers, suppliers or other related industries that do not have much of a presence in the region. It is important to find these gaps because they offer very good opportunities for business recruitment.

There are a number of reasons for this:

- **Highly attractive business environment**—outside companies that could come into a region and fill in these weaker subclusters will tend to view the business environment as highly attractive. The well-developed cluster indicates that within the region there are unique attributes that support that cluster's business (these attributes can only be identified through follow-on analysis). The fact that many firms succeed in the region over time creates an inherently attractive business environment for companies in the targeted subcluster;
- **Few head-to-head competitors**—were the company to come to the region, it would face few head-to-head local competitors. Because the subcluster is weak in the region, there would not be many other similar firms in the area;
- **Likelihood of success**—because the company would be coming into a well-established cluster, while at the same time facing few local competitors, it would be more likely to succeed. Unlike a company lured in by incentives, this company would come due to existing assets and sales opportunities; and
- **Strengthening cluster overall**—because the company would be filling in a gap in the cluster, it would help other companies in the region be more competitive, improving efficiency in goods and services access with the gap filled.

In short, a region can offer companies in these weak subclusters a compelling, highly differentiated value proposition—everything they need to compete, with little direct competition in the area. Using this type of analysis, SEZ administrators will be better prepared planning which industries and clusters will need workers; whether high-end activities will remain viable; whether manufacturing will remain competitive in the region; which potential and emerging clusters in the region can be successfully developed; and what factors will differentiate the region. Such a fact-based strategy also helps administrators and regional investors create broad-based consensus and action among the relevant leaders and institutions in the business, government, civic and education spheres.

In addition to enhancing the economic competitiveness of a region, by carrying out a meticulous subcluster analysis and working to fill gaps, the SEZ will be able to reduce its ecological footprint, reducing overall resource consumption. By co-locating elements within a supply chain, the SEZ will be able to improve product production efficiency while lowering the carbon emissions associated with transport and shipping.

Carbon Footprint

If changes are not made in terms of consumption patterns, energy provision and industrial efficiency, then the city is on a trajectory to have a carbon footprint of 20 tonnes per person by 2030, similar to the current U.S. average footprint. The "Low Carbon Trajectory" would mean the footprint would be 2.5 tonnes by 2030. Every year that the footprint rises, it becomes the more difficult to achieve significant reduction and change.

As an initial assessment of strategies below demonstrates, the effectiveness of a range of policies to reduce the carbon footprint can vary substantially. With the suggested changes, the footprint could be reduced from 9 to 5 tonnes.

The key intervention with the greatest reduction is renewable energy, achieving a reduction of 1.9 tonnes per capita.[19] While efficiency changes are continually occurring within industry, the "Efficient Industry" intervention represents an improvement beyond the standard change of efficiency that is currently about 1% a year. It is an immediate 20% shift in

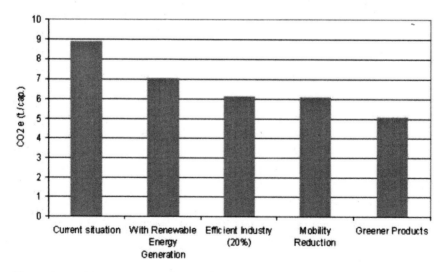

Figure 11.6 CO_2 emissions reduction from 2007 baseline (cumulative).

the average footprint per unit of economic output generated by industries within the city.[20]

A mobility reduction could result in a smaller impact. Finally, greener products include a shift in the consumer basket toward lower impact products. This includes all areas of consumption such as food, clothing, and electrical equipment. Consumers could be incentivized, perhaps through a VAT discount to purchase low-carbon and energy goods—so that manufacturers of goods are motivated to redesign their products to be more competitive. Consumption will also be reflected through a true, non-subsidized energy price that progressively has a carbon-impact price included. A similar 20% change is anticipated.

While the recommended 2.5 tonnes/capita may be difficult to reach and different for each situation, there are strategies, especially in the spatial and infrastructure sectors, to reduce carbon footprint. However, it should also include government and household behavior, and subsequent rebound effects of reduced energy use. In the current institutional setting, a low-carbon lifestyle is not sufficiently rewarded. If the pursuit of a SEZ is to ensure unlimited economic growth without any acknowledgment of bio-physical limits, then it simply cannot be called "sustainable." To become an SSEZ, SEZs will need to promote sustained growth with a low ecological footprint, with reduction strategies and the carbon footprint analysis.

Infrastructure and Spatial Planning

Based on the initial audit, the plan for infrastructure and spatial planning would include several interrelated strategies.

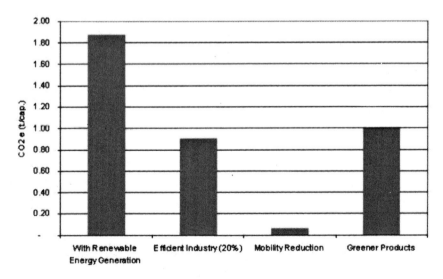

Figure 11.7   Potential reduction of individual interventions.

Generally, in most developing countries, walking, bicycling, and public transport take up the majority share, but as they become more prosperous, car ownership and usage rises. In understanding the transport plans, as income improves, the key is to maintain high levels of sustainable, low-emissions transport, considering increased vehicle movements and future developments, and prohibiting high-polluting vehicles. A carbon footprint reduction can best be achieved through the formation of a Low Emission Strategy (LES).[21] LES provides a package of measures to help mitigate the transport impacts of a development. Sample LES recommendations for SEZs include:

- Create an efficient, integrated external transport system to coordinate the development of railway, highway and canal transport.
- Establish a connecting transport system that includes light rail, bus, bicycle, etc., emphasizing car use as the last option.
- Coordinate the transport system in the industrial park and related urban areas, resulting in the SEZ becoming an organic part of the integrated transport system.
- Fuel the public transport system and private vehicles with renewables, including electric cars and motorcycles.
- Combine short- and long-term programs to help the transport system face challenges from development.
- Develop a strong education and communications platform to champion LES so that residents and visitors alike are knowledgable and supportive of the transport system[22].

Equally important is the question of land use and open space. In looking to enhance their sustainability, SEZs should cluster manufacturers using industrial symbiosis principles together with integrated supply chain management, emphasizing clean, green manufacturing practices. The resource cycle will direct location choices. Green infrastructure should integrate with the physical development of the whole zone. A large percentage of the total SSEZ area should be left as multifunctional countryside, for the purpose of improving health and well-being. The neighborhood design should link homes to business, commercial and community functions, connecting people to the places they want to go to.

Additionally, hard paved areas can be made porous to help refill aquifers and to slow down run-off. Improved water capture and gray water management in urban areas could provide reliable water supplies for irrigating farmland during drought conditions and help to maintain food productivity in climate change induced swings in climate. Water could be stored in lakes in urban parks as has been done in Curitiba, or could be cleaned using natural reed bed systems as has been done in Freiburg. Fitting water capture and grey water recycling systems into industries and homes can save household potable water consumption, reduce storm run-off, and curtail energy consumption.

As a final component to land use and open space, food security and CO_2 contribution issues can also be addressed within the built environment. A sustainable food distribution system based on national networks of regional, local and urban farms can lessen transport costs, the need for chemical fertilizers, all while strengthening rural-urban ties. Buildings can also produce food with artificial light, hydroponics and nutrient recycling from city waste. Access to local, healthy, seasonal produce can increase within the SSEZ. Finally, the improving building thermal and visualisation standards should also be taken advocated to maximize thermal comfort using natural conditions and lessen energy intensity.

An improvement to resource and waste management is also achievable by considering each stage of the development life cycle (see Figure 11.8), from the design to the end-of-life of buildings. The life cycle is split into five distinct phases (design, construction, operation, maintenance, and deconstruction) each occurring sequentially. By considering waste generation at

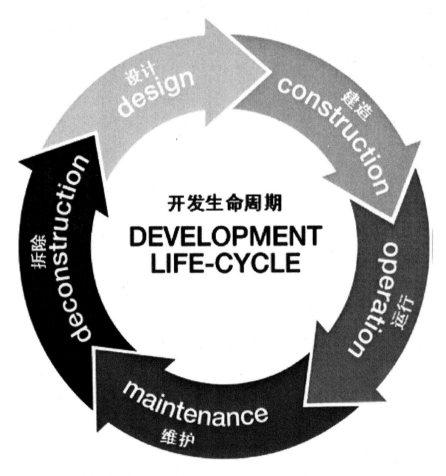

Figure 11.8 The development life cycle and resource and waste management.

each stage, SEZs will be better prepared to incorporate technical solutions such as better logistics for materials supply, designing out waste and better site practice to minimise wastage.

A site waste management plan can manage waste segregation, contain SMART[23] objectives (e.g., recycled content, % recover of waste), and include a material procurement, education and communications components. Additionally, a construction logistics plan should include material sourcing and waste removal.

With a high percentage of organic waste, a sustainable strategy would source separate organic waste from recyclables and residuals (three streams). The organic waste would then be combined with sewage sludge from the wastewater treatment plant and treated in an anaerobic digestion (AD) facility to produce biogas to generate electricity and heat. The dry recyclables would be sent off site for recycling, while the residual waste would be sent for thermal treatment at a gasification facility to produce a synthetic gas to generate electricity and heat. An example SEZ's domestic organic waste found that an anaerobic digestion facility could generate the following:

- 9,000,000 m³ of biogas
- 11.5 million kWh/year of electricity
- 18 million kWh/year of heat
- 1.4 MW/year of power
- 26,000 tonnes of digestate for fertilizer
- 190,000 m²/yr of power (heat and electricity)[24]

With strong spatial planning, built around industrial ecology, circular economy, and cyclical industry cluster concepts, the waste produced in one industry can be used as inputs for another industry. This exchange network is facilitated by the proximity of the different stakeholders. The integration of the residential community should also be encouraged. The opportunities for synergies within the zone can cover a large range of resources from byproduct material exchange to shared water or waste treatment infrastructure. These synergies are implemented because they enable costs savings for the participants in addition to reducing their environmental impact. Figure 11.9 illustrates different strategies that could be used to develop a circular economy.

Finally, energy and building fabric standards must be taken into account. SEZs can be ahead of the curve by enacting decarbonizing strategies. They should identify the scale of energy reductions achievable and seek to match the resulting energy needs to locally available renewable energy sources. Priority should be given to early investment to reducing energy needs, sourcing from renewable sources and reducing overall costs. New decarbonized communities will have less car usage, energy-efficient buildings, and local renewable energy generation.

Together, the strategies for the four impact areas will help transform the SEZ into an SSEZ. Current SEZs address each other separately, but by

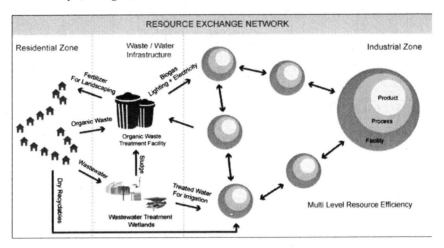

Figure 11.9   Illustration of resource exchange network.

integrating them around economic and environmental sustainability, the chances of reaching the environmental and economic goals, and successfully following the strategic plan greatly increases.

3. Ensure Alignment among Key Stakeholders

Once the plan is in place, the real transformation begins. Transforming an SEZ into an SSEZ will require a shift in policies and actions that extend across all sectors of the economy. To carry this out successfully, it is important that the institutions and individuals in charge of defining and implementing new policy and changed behaviors act under a shared consensus or agreement. Existing institutions can be leveraged, with relevant stakeholders coming together as a result of a shared sense of urgency to drive to decisive action.

Through its extant governing structure, an SEZ already has institutions and processes in place to support the necessary discussions that will lead to alignment among stakeholders. This may include processes that ensure alignment between local, regional, and national governments. Even with certain alignment processes in place, an SEZ may find it necessary to establish new institutions or processes in order to address components of the strategic plan that may never have been considered in the past.

4. Monitor and Report Progress

Mechanisms to monitor and report progress are necessary to measure success and identify areas that require new or reformed policies. By highlighting areas of success, progress reports provide SEZ administrators an opportunity to learn best practices that may be applicable to other elements of the strategic plan. Areas of lagging development provide data that equip an administrator to draft new policies or define necessary adjustments to resource investments.

An SEZ must monitor its progress by defining metrics for each of the elements of its strategic plan. These metrics should consist of both qualitative and quantitative measurements; a shift toward solely one or the other risks the loss of relevant details that can inform future policies.

By following the four steps outlined against each of the four impact areas, an SEZ can begin taking the tangible measures toward sustainability and becoming an SSEZ. The SEZ customizes definitions of the impact areas and then moves from aspirations to action items through the four steps. This shift from theoretical to actionable sets the stage for long-term growth prospects that can improve the well-being of the SSEZ population.

CONCLUSION

This chapter has outlined the importance of sustainable development within an economic zone, from both an economic and environmental standpoint. It certainly has not and does not aim to address the finer details. But it is a start of a much needed and critical discussion in an unexplored area that has many possibilities to further economic and environmental sustainability. Much more needs and will be done, but the process has to begin, and a path is shown first through this strategy chapter on the transformation to become SSEZs.[25]

An SEZ that seeks to attract investment, create jobs and improve its built environment must recognize the way in which smart and efficient environmental policies should be incorporated with an aspiration for a high quality of life and economic competitiveness. Achieving environmental sustainability cannot be seen as half-heartedly implementing policies that are measured in onerous costs and taxes. Likewise, driving economic competitiveness must be seen as linked to—rather than at odds with—environmental sustainability.

Becoming an SSEZ is truly about defining competitive advantages. This can be done in the context of improving the existing legal, regulatory and governance frameworks of current SEZs, which would mean a minimal disruption, low additional implementation costs and swift change. Economically, an SEZ that takes a cluster-based approach to innovate and differentiate itself will continuously be poised to develop—thereby ensuring continued investment and growth. Environmentally, an SEZ that seeks to develop energy-efficient infrastructure, improve waste management techniques and create a sustainable way of living will have a unique and compelling story to attract investors, workers and residents alike.

Further, the potential to lower one's carbon footprint is enormous; imagine if this process were to take place in all of China's SEZs—19% of the world's SEZs, with more than 50 million employees total[26]—or the rest of the world's SEZs. The transformation for the world's SEZs to become SSEZs presents an unprecedented opportunity to economically and environmentally improve our way of life now and for generations to come.

The world is experiencing crisis on both an economic and environmental front. But this is also an opportunity to re-think how to best develop our economies and nurture our environment, and SEZs are uniquely positioned to serve as leading examples for ways that economic competitiveness can be coupled with, rather than in opposition to, environmental consciousness. A crisis presents many perils, but it also opens the door for opportunity. SEZ administrators can decide to drive economic development, improve the living standards of those within the zone and proportionally lower the impact on the environment. SEZs have the opportunity to once again serve as demonstration areas for astounding, historic success—this time by showcasing the ability to link economic growth with environmental sustainability. It is at this moment that SEZs can position themselves for long-term success, and become SSEZs.

NOTES

1. *Sustainable development of special economic zones in emerging markets,* Grail Research, Monitor Group, 2009.
2. *This can't last: Study ranks countries by environmental sustainability,* LiveScience, 2005.
3. Renewable energy use to be made mandatory for SEZ's, *The Financial Express,* June 2009; New-age tech to power Faridabad's green 'SEZ', *The Times of India,* November 2008; *Regulations of the Shenzhen special economic zone on the environmental protection of construction projects,* Shanzen Municipal Office of Legislative Affairs, July 2006; *Special economic zones and competitiveness,* Asian Development Bank, November 2007; *Green building to the United Arab Emirates,* the Australian Government website, March 2009; *Dubai International Academic City Phase-III becomes Middle East's first and largest LEED certified academic facility,* Zawya, June 2009; *ITT signs MoU with GreenSpaces,* Merinews, March 2008.
4. Clusters are geographically proximate groups of interconnected companies and associated institutions in a particular field, linked by commonalities and complementarities. Clusters are normally contained within a geographic area where ease of communication and interaction is possible. Clusters cut across traditional industry classifications. Clusters take various forms depending on their sophistication, the field of activity, location and historical roots. Developed clusters, however, normally include end-product or service companies; suppliers of specialized inputs, components, machinery and services; financial institutions; and firms in related industries. Clusters also often include firms in downstream industries; producers of complementary products; specialized infrastructure providers; government and other institutions providing specialized training, education, information, research, and technical support; and standard setting agencies. Finally, many clusters include trade associations and other collective private sector bodies that support cluster members.

5. *Clusters of innovation, regional foundations of U.S. competitiveness*, Monitor Group and Professor Michael E. Porter, Harvard University, 2001.

6. *Special economic zones*, FIAS, April 2008 SEZs are an umbrella term for many other types of free zones, which have certain characteristics in common. These include geographically delineated area that is legally defined and often physically enclosed; a single management/administration for that geographic area; eligibility for benefits among consumers and businesses physically located within the area; and separate customs area for import/export that includes streamlined procedures and limited documentation requirements.

7. "SEZs: engine derailed?", www.indiatogether.org, January 2009.

8. "India's tryst with special economic zones", www.opinionasia.org, August 2006.

9. *Does trade lead to a race to the bottom in environmental standards? Another look at the issues*, Philippine Institute for Development Studies, October 2005.

10. *Special economic zones*, FIAS, April 2008.

11. *Greening growth: How local government can build the green economy.*

12. *What is good governance?* United Nations Economic and Social Commission for Asia and the Pacific, 2009.

13. Ibid.

14. *Clusters of innovation, regional foundations of U.S. competitiveness*, Monitor Group, and Professor Michael E. Porter, Harvard University, 2001.

15. For further information on how to assess a region's climate for entrepreneurship, see *Pathways to prosperity*, Monitor Group, 2009. An electronic copy can be obtained through www.compete.monitor.com.

16. Carbon footprint was chosen as the main indicator for environmental sustainability because it is easier to quantify, compare and define. It is also internationally recognized and accepted; it is the main indicator for governmental climate change and environmental discussions; however, there are other indicators that can be used.

17. Barrett, J., Paul, A., Scott, K., & Dawkins, E. (2009). Counting consumption. WWF-UK.

18. Benyus, J. (1997). *Biomimicry*. New York: HarperCollins.

19. This intervention assumes a 100% renewable electricity supply for the city and does not cover heat, only power.

20. Both renewable and energy-efficiency strategies are discussed in more detail in the previous spatial and infrastructure section and need to be considered for both costs and carbon concerns, specific to the local context.

21. The primary aim of LES is to accelerate the uptake of low emission fuels and technologies in and around a development site. This usually takes the form of an area where some kind of enforcement is carried out to ensure particular types of vehicles are restricted. Some UK authorities are already making effective use of LES. LES are secured through a combination of planning conditions and legal obligations. They may incorporate policy measures and/or require financial investments in and contributions to the delivery of low emission transport projects and plans, including strategic monitoring and assessment activities. LES differs from a LEZ (Low Emission Zone) which refers to a geographic area where emissions from road transport are mitigated. A LEZ may be one aspect of an LES in an area.

22. Optimized real-time journey planning can transform safety and ease of public transport use and improve service interchange. Information would be available over hand-held devices and at kiosks within all service locations. Operators would have the advantage of having passengers guided around breakdown points, and feedback would enable service interchange to be improved. This service would make public transport as, if not more,

desirable as private car transport. The whole system could be powered by solar energy including the handsets of the users.

23. Specific, Measurable, Achievable, Realistic and Time-related.
24. This assumes that most internal areas match the Chinese National Code GB50189 energy use standard of 160 kWh/m²/yr.
25. This chapter acknowledges that there are certain topics that may need to be further addressed before an SEZ administrator can begin to successfully outline a customized plan to become an SSEZ. These include SEZ-specific areas not discussed or analyzed in the chapter, such as production- and consumption-based accounts, supply chain flows, product life cycle, behavioral/cultural issues (e.g., entrenched attitudes of residents and workers) that may prevent barriers to change, unique political situations, and specific subcluster analyses that reveal the drivers behind a region's strong clusters.
26. World Bank, April 2008, p. 27.

BIBLIOGRAPHY

Abelaira, A. (2004, December). Ireland's economic miracle: What is the Celtic tiger? *Celtic Countries Magazine.*
Ahmedabad, A. N. (2008, November 4). New-age tech to power Faridabad's Green SEZ. *The Times of India.*
Allen, N. (2008, June 9). Copenhagen named world's best city for quality of life by Monocle Magazine. *Telegraph.*
Austrian Government (2009, March). Green building to the United Arab Emirates'. Retrieved from http://www.austrade.gov.au/Green-building-to-the-United-Arab-Emirates/default.aspx.
Barrett, J., Paul, A., Scott, K., & Dawkins, E. (2009). Counting consumption. Godalming, Surrey: WWF-UK.
BBC News (2006, January 9). China lifts annual growth figures. Retrieved from http://news.bbc.co.uk/1/hi/business/4594132.stm.
CSEP (2008). Fact sheet: China emerging as new leader in clean energy policies, China sustainable energy program. Retrieved from http://www.efchina.org/.
Crafts, N., & Toniolo, G. (Eds.) (1996). *Economic growth in Europe since 1945.* Cambridge: Cambridge University Press.
Deheng, S. (2006). Special economic zones and economic growth in China. Address by H. E. Mr. Song Deheng, Consul General of the People's Republic of China, Conference on Special Economic Zones: Growth Drivers of Maharashtra, Mumbai, June 5.
EPA (2000, April). Ireland's environment—A millennium report (Environmental Protection Agency).
Esty, D. C., & Winston, A. S. (2009). *Green to gold: How smart companies use environmental strategy to innovate, create value, and build competitive advantage.* Hoboken, NJ: John Wiley & Sons.
Esty, D. C., Levy, M., Kim., C., de Sherbinin, A., Srebotnjak, T., & Mara, V. (2008). *2008 environmental performance index.* New Haven, CT: Yale Center for Environmental Law and Policy and Palisades, NY: Center for International Earth Science Information Network (CIESIN), Columbia University. Retrieved from http://epi.yale.edu/.
Feng, Y., & Guo, W. (2007, November). *Special economic zones and competitiveness.* Asian Development Bank, Pakistan Resident Mission, Series No. 2. Retrieved from http://www.adb.org/Documents/Reports/PRM-Policy-Notes/Special-Economic-Zone-Shenzhen.pdf.

Financial Express (2009, June 16). Renewable energy use to be made mandatory for SEZs. Retrieved from http://www.financialexpress.com/news/renewable-energy-use-to-be-made-mandatory-for-sezs/477037/.

Findlay, M., & Preston, F. (2008, October). Low carbon zones: A transformational agenda for China and Europe. London: Chatham House.

Foreign Investment Advisory Service (2008, April). *Special economic zones: Performance, lessons learned, and implications for zone development.* Washington, DC: The World Bank Group.

Ge, W. (1999), *Special economic zones and the economic transition in China.* Singapore: World Scientific.

Goswami, B. (2007, February 14). Lessons from China—Special Export Zones—SEZ. *In Motion Magazine.*

Grant, B. (2003, April). *Traditional regulation vs. performance based regulation.* Vancouver: BC Utilities Commission.

Junior Luwang, N. G. (2008, February 8). Special economic zones in India suffer from policy flaws. *The Economic Times.*

Kasturi, K. (2009, January 15). SEZs: Engine derailed. *India Together.*

Lewin, T. (2008, February 11). In oil-rich Mideast, shades of the Ivy League. *New York Times.*

Liu, X., Heilig, G. K., Chen, J., & Heino, M. (2007). Interactions between economic growth and environmental quality in Shenzhen, China's first special economic zone. *Ecological Economics, 62,* 559–70.

LiveScience (2005, January). This can't last: Study ranks countries by environmental sustainability. Retreived from http://www.livescience.com/environment/050128_environment_ranking.html

Mau, V. (2004, March). *Post-revolution consolidation.* Washington, D.C.: Center for Defense Information.

MacDonald, G. M., Beilman, D. W., Kremenetski, K. V., Sheng, Y., Smith, L. C., & Velichko, A. A. (2006). Rapid early development of circumarctic peatlands and atmospheric CH_4 and CO_2 variations. *314,* 285–8.

Medalla, E. M., & Lazaro, D. C. (2005, October). Does trade lead to a race to the bottom in environmental standards? Another look at the issues (Philippine Institute for Development Studies, Discussion Paper No. 2005–23).

Merinews (2008, March). ITT signs MoU with GreenSpaces. Retrieved from http://www.merinews.com/catFull.jsp?articleID=131006.

Monitor Group (2009a, January), *Paths to prosperity: Promoting entrepreneurship in the 21st century.* Retrieved from http://www.compete.monitor.com/App_Themes/MRCCorpSite_v1/DownloadFiles/NED_report_final.pdf.

———(2009b). *Sustainable development of special economic zones in emerging markets.* Grail Research.

Morgan Stanley (2006, June). Indian economics: The SEZ rush. Morgan Stanely Research Asia-Pacific.

Ota, T. (2003a, March). Industrial policy in transitional economy: The role of China's special economic zone in economic development. Retrieved from http://www.toyo.ac.jp.

———(2003b, March). The role of special economic zones in China's economic development as compared with Asian export processing zones: 1979–1995. Retrieved from http://www.iae.univ-poitiers.fr/.

Porter, M. E., & Monitor Group (2001). *Clusters of innovation: Regional foundations of U.S. competitiveness.* Washington, D.C.: Council on Competitiveness.

Press Release Network (2002, May). Technology park announced for Dubai. Retrieved from http://www.pressreleasenetwork.com/pr-2002/may/mainpr1240.htm.

Project Monitor (2006, June 19). China's amazing SEZs. Retrieved from http://www.projectmonitor.com/detailnews.asp?newsid=11583.

Richerzhagen, C., von Frieling, T., Hansen, N., Minnaert, A., Netzer, N., & Russ-bild, J. (2008). *Energy efficiency in buildings in China: Policies, barriers and opportunities.* Bonn: German Development Institute.

Schuller, J. K. (2007, October). Transfer of ideas from research to industry: The case of the United States of America (University of Florida).

Shanzen Municipal Office of Legislative Affairs (2006, July). Regulations of the Shenzhen special economic zone on the environmental protection of construction projects. Retrieved from http://fzj.sz.gov.cn/en/285.asp.

Shao, M., Yang, X., Zhang, Y., & Li, W. (2006). City clusters in China: Air and surface water pollution. *Frontiers in Ecology and the Environment, 4,* 353–61.

Singh, A. S. (2006, August). India's tryst with special economic zones. Retrieved from www.opinionasia.org.

Stephenson, M. (2007). Topic brief: Economic development and the quality of legal institutions, Department of Government and Law School, Harvard University. Retrieved from http://siteresources.worldbank.org/INTLAWJUSTINST/Resources/LegalInstitutionsTopicBrief.pdf.

Upadhyaya, H. (2008, June 23). CAG indicts SEZ policy. *India Together.*

World Bank (2008, April). *Special Economic Zones: Performance, lessons learned, and implications for zone development.* Washington, DC: World Bank. Available online at: http://www.ifc.org/ifcext/fias.nsf/AttachmentsByTitle/SEZpaperdiscussion/$FILE/SEZs+report_April2008.pdf

Wu, C-T. (1985). China's special economic zones: Five years after. *Asian Journal of Public Administration, 7,* 127–43.

Yoo, S. J. (2003, August). Incentive-based environmental policies in Korea (Korea Energy Economics Institute).

Zawya (2009, June 23). Dubai International Academic City Phase-III becomes Middle East's first and largest LEED certified academic facility. Press release. .

FURTHER RESOURCES

Databases

China Census Bureau
Economist Intelligence Unit
Hebei Statistical Bureau
Ministry of Commerce, China
Suzhou City Census Bureau
Suzhou City Statistical Yearbook
World Development Indicators database, World Bank

Websites

CHINA.ORG.CN
China-Singapore Suzhou Industrial Park Development Co., official website
China-Singapore Suzhou Industrial Park, official website
EChinaCities.com
Friends of the Irish Environment, official website
Green Valley Industrial Park, official website
Saudi Arabia General Investment Authority, official website
Shannon Development, company website
Suzhou City official website

12 Considering Green Business and Green Values

J. C. Spender

WHAT DO WE KNOW?

Our conference program's segmentation into issues, challenges and solutions implies some agreement about how to engage "green issues" and proceed toward a "Green New Deal." Whether we consider energy management, oceanic acidity, the fall in the water table or the end of the age of oil, our target is to find politically viable, socially acceptable and ecologically sustainable agricultural, industrial and social policies that cohere into an integrated way of being. Prince Charles's 2009 Dimbleby Lecture reaffirms this. Hard though this project might be, it seems one around which we should surely all gather.

Nonetheless I shall take a different position and argue it would be wiser to begin by admitting we have no idea what we are doing. This is not to insult the many now working passionately on green issues; rather, it is about clarifying the distinction between knowing and acting that lies at the core of our eco age's challenge. With no policy position or revenue stream to protect, I am institutionally free to suggest our present "crisis" has less to do with the presence or absence of appropriate policies about energy, public health or fish stocks than with how we think about matters green. Beneath the debates about what "the science" does or does not show, or how we might resolve the North-South or Rich-Poor differentials, I shall argue that we are in the grip of an epistemological crisis that runs deeper than any crisis of technology, politics or ecology.

Green problems have a special sharpness because they force us to look into the state of our knowledge about who we are and how we interact through what we do to our world. We are reminded of how much we do not know about this—such as global warming or the ecology of the deep oceans. My starting-out assertion is that we are confronting a historical break in how we understand the world and here I agree with the Prince, an authority one might not normally cite. Strained circumstances make for strange bedfellows. So I shall divert from our conference's title—"Green Business and Green Values"—to reflect on "green" itself, its meaning and how it challenges our ways of understanding.

At one level, of course, the suggestion that we have lost our way might strike some as a reason to turn toward religion, as evident in the Pope Benedict's third encyclical. Many of those grappling with corporate social responsibility, capitalism's contradictions, medical ethics, sweated labor, the prospect of water and pollution wars and so on are moving in this direction, lamenting our age's loss of religion's moral compass. Engaging this calls for more knowledge, study and reflection than I can possibly bring to the task so I shall look at a narrower issue and suggest a new constructive role for philosophers and social science academics.

These quiet laborers, merely thinking about thinking, often find themselves positioned against activists, energetic business people and policymakers whose primary focus is action—stop talking and do something! But thinking is full of pitfalls, and we need thoughtful action, not knee-jerk responses or action for the sake of appearing active. No doubt the widespread urge to act, to establish carbon trading or tighten fleet mileage or gas emission standards will prove irresistible; it certainly salves our anxieties even as we wonder about the intended and unintended outcomes. That is the politicians' problem. Ecology has appeared on their menu and they must take a position if they are to earn their constituents' support. Academics are not in this situation and must wonder what, if anything, they might bring to the table from their ivory aeries. They might, for instance, wonder at the disappearance of the religious and philosophical frameworks within which green issues would have been discussed 150 or more years ago. I shall argue time is crucial and in losing our way we have also lost track of our time.

BACK TO THE FUTURE

We live in the shadow of the Victorian Age. Inter alia it gave us the modern university's agenda and science as the privileged mode of knowing, standing against previous times' less objective modes—religion, politics, feudal relations, and so on. Science's promise was that it would provide each of us the freedom to discover the truth for ourselves, free of intervention or interference by others. But most thinkers appreciated that science's victory was far from complete, even as we hesitated to admit it; it seemed to overlook much about human knowing. The developments of pragmatism, existentialism and various forms of post-positive modernism reinforced and articulated these doubts. In the UK the popular appeal of CP Snow's 1959 Rede lecture about "the two cultures" made it academically acceptable to say we had two legitimate modes of thinking and knowing. The point being that while the conflict or relationship between science and the humanities remains unresolved—in a philosophical or methodological sense—at least their differences were no longer hidden under a carpet of Victorian dogma. Nor did the humanities need to be grovelingly apologetic as they were in the late 1800s. Nor was pluralism to be considered mere methodological weakness, though justifying and handling it remains a challenge.

Notwithstanding these advances, many academic disciplines seem unwilling to respond to their message, especially those focused on social policy and collective human action. Shying at the methodological chasm, they typically pursue one or other way of knowing, rather than working to bridge between and embrace both—as we see from the ongoing debates about quantitative and qualitative research methods. Likewise some philosophers—perhaps spurred by Snow's agenda—continue to seek an overarching mode of human knowing that, if found, would surely have a significant part to play in how we might deal with green issues. But we now suspect this methodological Nirvana is forever out of reach and the Victorian dream of total objectivity and universal laws no more than a fogged reflection of Plato's hunches. In the meantime we must confront our situation and make haste to cut away anything that stands in the way of our grasping Gaia more securely. We have nothing but our knowledge to bring to this task. Although our capacity for action is profoundly human, it is only acceptable when shaped by our knowledge. This is my point—do we really know enough about our situation to think the green project is about choosing between identifiable actions?

THE PLACE OF DOUBT

I mentioned religion because some of the deepest disagreements among Europeans during the Age of Enlightenment were around the limits to human knowing, specifically about whether we were imprisoned by "radical doubt" or could ever achieve certainty or "God's Eye View." The ancient religious, humbler than we, presumed not, that it was not given to us to know the way the gods knew. Acceptance of radical doubt—what we might now call "bounded rationality"—was central for Descartes and Kant, and yet, in some mysterious way, Victorian science forgot it. We became persuaded the scientific method of Bacon and Newton could be developed sufficiently to let us achieve "objective truth." So my chapter's main message is that we might leverage pre-modern doubt into our thinking about today's situation and see more clearly how, in many ways, we are the product and prisoners of Victorian ways of thinking. As long as we continue to deny doubt and thus the shortcomings in how we know, we shall remain trapped in the Victorians' ultimately ineffective ways of thinking. Green means challenging such naïve thinking.

Bounded rationality is a way of defining who we are. It reminds us we can never find out everything that must be understood if we are to achieve even the tiniest degree of certainty. We are also limited in our abilities to grasp the implications of the knowledge we have already developed. Following Popper's popularization, natural science articulated bounded rationality as the method of falsifiable hypotheses about our future experience (Popper, 1969). Scientific statements should not aspire to be fully certain knowledge of the world, simply close enough to be practical and useful as we act within it. The approved methods of science would produce knowledge that would be reasonably coherent without being in any sense complete. While our knowledge must be shaped by how we humans know, Kant's point, the deeper question of how the result might relate to the world remains unconsidered. Thus, thinking about global warming is not at all the same thing as acting by, say, reducing carbon dioxide emissions in the expectation of changing it. Acting engages the world in ways quite different from thinking through the way we have modeled it. The passive and active modes of knowing—as in Ryle's distinction between knowing-that and knowing-how (Ryle, 1954)—can only converge when we have a complete model of reality, when we have reached beyond our bounded rationality to the place of total knowing. The Victorian dream was that science could be an apparatus like Jacob's ladder that would help us escape our condition of radical doubt and reach this place. Yet, if we care to look, we can see the futility of thinking this way, of looking to science to fix a situation we are creating through our application of science.

The humanities are in a different position; they lack a coherent method or even agreement about how one can know. On the one hand, we have various "historical methods" that range from truth as revealed by the accumulation of historical facts, such as a royal lineage or the sequence of events in a revolution, to the adoption of explanatory paradigms such as the inevitability of a people rising against a feudal power or the impact of acquiring a new military technology. Beneath these different notions of explanation are un-resolvable questions about how to justify the analyst's interpretation and selection, for science's ceteris paribus is not available. We cannot put history in the laboratory, extracting it from life and the unknown multitude of alternative explanations of every human event. Thus, the humanities suggest forms of knowing forever contingent on arbitrary selections of the facts and causal attributions, and, unlike science, they lack the methodological apparatus necessary to prove things could not have been otherwise.

So I shall take Snow at his word and contrast our two current ways of knowing—for it is in such ambiguity that we must act mindfully. Note that science and the humanities only seem to be different ways of knowing because we are denied full knowledge. Were certainty available, we would not need even one research methodology. Consciousness itself would be enough, for the Truth would expose itself to us without interference or delay. Our research methods are our various strategies for dealing with our particular modes of not knowing and the resulting inaccessibility of the Truth. It follows, as social studies of science have shown as they rediscover Kant's critiques and erode the Victorian dream, that our knowledge is never "of the world" or of the things we seek to know. Knowledge is always about our own project—making a life and living in the world as we find it. We see that science is one of the humanities after all—inevitably humanist and imprisoned in how we think, forever tied up with subjective interpretations that can never be grounded in an out-of-life "objectivity." While philosophers and epistemologists may be excited by exploring how one way of knowing or discovering relates to another or might be better justified and so preferred, the immediate practical issue is to handle the doubt that is the most pressing characteristic of our present situation.

Most understand bounded rationality in psychological terms, the consequence of our limited neural capabilities. But it is also about our relationship to the things beyond the mind that we seek to know. A different way of addressing the same apparent disjunction between our outer and inner worlds is to restate the fundamental difficulties that arise when we discover ourselves located within the system we are trying to know, making it impossible to put it at arm's length and view it objectively. Just as we cannot achieve certainty so we have no access to that Archimedean fulcrum from which we might survey reality.

Here is the fundamental challenge of dealing with matters green—we are embedded within them, part of the problem and its imagined solutions, in a Wonderland of our own time and making. The epistemological consequence is that until we abandon the pursuit of certainty and objectivity, and the curious dream of being able to stand outside this world, we shall never find our way to the lived heart of our situation and explore possibilities that are not mere masks covering its interactions—such as "climate-gate" and the debates about the problematic "science" of global warming illustrate.

Gore continues to do a fine job proposing recent changes in temperature, ice cover, and vegetation are proof positive of our messing up the biosphere (Gore, 1993). But how can we ever know whether this is correct or not? We cannot conduct a "natural experiment" on the human condition. So the question is Does it matter? To settle it, we would need a complete validated model of the universe and/or access to that Archimedean fulcrum. Gore is neither a fool nor naïve and knows he is a perishable influence around the world, so what is he really doing? I suspect he is deliberately challenging our belief that we have to get the science right before we can act responsibly, knowing that traps us into inaction as we wait for complete knowledge. But what are the alternatives? Is "the science" all we have to go on?

The problem here is not relativism, the bogeyman positivists deploy to de-legitimate the humanities' ways of knowing. Rather, the deeper challenge it is to grasp that fact that the discussion is about our condition, about how we know and act. There is irony here for Popper's motivations were as much political as philosophical, as his Open Society project revealed (Popper, 1945). While the knowledge that interested him—as a philosopher of science - was of the non-human, of what lay beyond the humanities, he actually envisaged a science-based democracy. As we wait for that to emerge, we wonder how to justify choices of human action under the conditions of rampant uncertainty and knowledge-absence that are so evident on matters green. We know we do not have the time or opportunity to act only on the basis of adequately established science, even though there are times it can be informative. Rather we face immediate choices about whether to intervene or not in a world we do not understand. Under these circumstances, if we choose to act, we are morally obliged to surface the interests involved. In other words, while we cannot know the consequences of our action, we can for sure try to find out who is likely to be impacted, who and where are those others who make up the human network. Cotton subsidies in the United States affect others in nations far away. Green means uncovering the ways in which such interactions work, it means building workable models of human society rather than of the natural world. It means adopting a humanist kind of pragmatism rather than a de-humanized positivism of "the real."

In the absence of certain knowledge and the rigorous plans that can be built on it, we have a Snow's pluralism, two immiscible ways of knowing—a scientific way and a humanities way. What happens here? As we admit this, we draw our choosing and acting out of the imagined impersonal world of facts and into the community of those acting and those affected, the very opposite of appealing to "scientific experts" who tell us they have some privileged access to a neutral objectivity beyond the lived world. Gore's strategy becomes clearer. He is not playing the scientist who thinks he knows reality; on the contrary, he is a canny politician working to re-shape the global warming discourse and thereby engage interest groups all too often excluded by the discourse of science. He recasts global warming as a political/social problem, reaffirming the ancient Greek belief that in the absence of certain knowledge all we have is democratic conversation. It alone must synthesize the pluralism within the situational contingencies the discussants are experiencing, allowing them to search for and find a consensus that reaffirms their membership of a single community. Conversation is the crucial process of constructing our experience and sense of self. Given bounded rationality, we have nothing else, weak as it might seem.

WHAT HAPPENED TO OUR CONVERSATION?

Around 150 years ago the European public conversation changed. The Newtonian model of natural science as the paradigmatic mode of knowing finally delegitimized an older tradition, the ancient art of rhetoric and persuasion that hinged on the philosophical modesty mentioned earlier. Rhetoric differs from logic alone precisely because it is fashioned around shared human situations in which proof and complete knowledge are not available. Reasonable agreement or *pisteis* was the objective—what lives on today as "beyond reasonable doubt." The Greeks were sharply aware their city-states could not function without such agreement and the collaborative action that could result. Their leaders could not claim or demonstrate certainty about the outcome of the action called for, even more important when it involved giving up a measure of self-interest in favor of the group. Note that rhetoric is about collaborative human action, not merely about propaganda and shaping opinion, reasoned action's precursors. We realize Greek communal activity, the Olympics, the drama, and so on, were laboratories for their rhetoric, and thereby the creation of the state. From several hundred years BCE through to the 18th century, rhetoric was one of three parts of the *trivium*, the central plank in European university education and academic scholarship (Conley, 1990). Adam Smith, for instance, was a professor of rhetoric long before there was economics. Green is about our need for a new rhetoric with which to create a new state of our world.

As soon as we emerge from the Victorian dream encapsulated in Lord Kelvin's dictum that "if you cannot measure it, you cannot improve it," we see science itself is no more than a family of rhetorical devices, a trope, a mode of persuasion that has achieved remarkable weight in spite of being, like every other discourse, ultimately founded on mere assumption. At this point Snow's two cultures collapse into one, that of the human conversation among the engaged. Green matters must be grasped from the subjective humanist point of view, from within our form of life, not as matters of science considered from an imagined objectivist point of view, beyond our life-world. Nature is not something to be understood as a "thing-in-itself" but as the inanimate that mediates the ways in which we (and the animate) impact each other. The epistemological re-positioning makes green rhetoric very different from the objective discourse of a science far removed from our experience and day-to-day life—the nature of black holes, say, or what were the causes of the Second World War? Green matters are about us, inherently indexical, constrained within the here and now and how we occupy and make our world. The key choice is always that between our action and inaction, between agency and acceptance or irresponsibility.

We cannot bring this constructive immediacy into our discourse until we have a sense of what is to be acted on. Mere abstractions will not do. Nor can we swallow the whole world in a single gulp. From medieval times through to Talcott Parsons we have been tempted to disaggregate human society into functional layers (Figure 12.1). While we experience ourselves

148   *J. C. Spender*

as individuals, we sense levels of analysis and possible action "above" and "below" us. Simon, who deserves more attention, saw society as "partially" decomposable (Simon, 1981). There is policy at the level of the family, China's "one child policy," or at the level of the industry, carbon trading. There is the level of sovereign nations and international agencies to demand they control their industries' emissions through their own national legislative processes. In general, we need a model functionally relevant to the action modes of the socio-political situation. Again, this asserts no certain knowledge of how human society functions, it is simply a reflection of social action heuristics we have generated over time.

Figure 12.1 suggests it makes sense to disaggregate any green action to a specific layer. Then we can evaluate it against criteria such as: (a) is there enough understanding for us to consider the decision reasoned, (b) is there the political will to carry the action through, and (c) can we anticipate the consequences sufficiently to reinforce (a) and (b) and can we see where the chips will fall, who will be impacted and how? We live within democratic capitalism, national and increasingly global, and business organizations are some of the most powerful and complex engines producing the goods and services we value. But business is bounded within a context of social, political and legal constraints. Clearly if business is to really engage green, rather than merely highjack its language to benefit its shareholders, its efforts to maximize shareholder wealth must be curbed by the public and the institutions created to implement their conclusions. But it is even more sharply bounded by its rhetoric, what can and cannot be said.

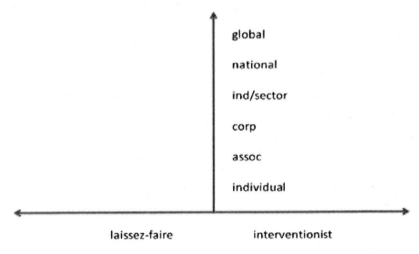

Figure 12.1   Field of green.

CONSIDERING RHETORIC AND POLITICAL ACTION

While rhetoric is more art than science, it benefits from several thousand years of thought about how we humans influence each other. First, there is the matter of identifying one's audience and what they are prepared to hear versus what seems incomprehensible or immediately unacceptable. This shapes the specifics of what might be said, its "tropes," the particular language, metaphors, metonyms, and parts of speech and the specific arguments to be brought to the persuasive task. Gore's process is rhetorically rich fully appreciating how his choice of media shapes the audience and what can be said. His deft use of scientific language distances him from pronouncing on "values," clothing his discourse in a contemporary authority a religious vocabulary, for instance, might lack. Yet his allusion to our responsibilities to future generations raises such issues, especially for so religiously inclined an audience as the United States. Likewise PowerPoint and projected graphics were not available to Cicero or Winston Churchill, but are available and acceptable in our age.

The overall project then is to reframe green matters as the most important and pressing for our collective consideration and to frame them with a language that enables us all to take part in a democratic discussion about our future. Implicit is the caution that such matters should not be left to elected representatives, for their political situation and compromises reduce their inclination and ability to properly engage the issues. Nor should they be captured by science. Can the public reclaim the green discourse as feminists have shown women must claim the discourse of their bodies? What are we really trying to do? Green is about action under uncertain circumstances not about developing better knowledge—the ultimately fatal temptation to inaction. To reclaim the discourse we must bring it to the same level of immediate engagement that we have with the rest of our everyday lives—fetching the children from school, calling on friends when they are sick, deciding to take up a new fitness project, and so on. Gore, as one person trying to show us how to proceed, is encouraging us to realize the contextualized nature of our lives and to embrace its implications responsibly and with moral commitment.

Rhetoric is about language applied to persuasion, not just verbal language, of course, but symbolic communication of all types. The language of science has proved extraordinarily compelling for two centuries, but it cannot be sufficient under our present circumstances of bounded rationality. Much of the science that deals with everyday matters, such as genetic engineering or ending life-support, has severed itself from the public discourse, creating a deep practical form of communal not-knowing that calls for the development of a new discourse around medical ethics—a new language with which we can engage the medics whose discipline-driven choices have little attachment to our individual existences yet affect them greatly. In the past, families and tribes addressed these questions as matters of social tradition; there were no disengaged specialists standing outside the group.

Green issues likewise demand a language of the engaged. How should we speak with the North-Western Pacific tribes about whale hunting, part of their culture but not of ours? Or with Chinese industrialists about acid rain as they struggle to put that country's impoverished past behind it, a past we do not share? Or with Western states' cattlemen about gaseous emissions as we dine on vegetables flown in from Israel? Without a mutual functioning language, we can have no reasonable persuasion and no collectively arrived-at action. The alternative is some form of science-based anti-democracy that, aside from anything else, implies a significant narrowing of the interests engaged and a temptation to totalitarian sub-optimality.

The argument here is that green issues are, by definition, those of the collectively and subjectively lived world and therefore inherently political—not scientific. Attempts to present them as about the objective world—especially that presumed in positivistic science—are no more than the charged rhetoric of disdain for those whose interests are being silenced. Green matters and how we think about them must be put into in a global political context in which all are entitled to be engaged, whatever their life-world. That is obviously a political statement, reminding us of the impossibility of addressing these issues in a non-political way and that attempts to present them as objectively science-driven are simply political moves to control the conversation.

POSSIBLE LANGUAGES

But before closing this chapter on "it's all politics, isn't it"—clearly true—we might return to the question of possible languages. The Western modes of thought evident in Snow's contrast of cultures are not widely shared around the world. Huntington's book (2003), whatever its merits, reminds us of Islamic culture and thought and its marked differences from Western thought. Any global conversation about green issues must take alternative ways of thinking into account, just as it must take Indian, Chinese and Filipino thinking and culture into account—and a lot more peoples' cultures besides. Perhaps academe's most significant challenge is to do this language work and thereby help enlarge the discourse, rather than leave it to the politicians of the moment. In short, green issues challenge us to globalize academe and so marshal the human race's knowledge resources in ways that have not been imagined since the Abbasid translation project and its attempts to codify the Book of Human Knowledge (Gutas, 1998).

Nor is the Western situation as simple as Snow suggests. Since Victorian times and the noted contrast between scientific objectivity and subjective interpretation, the public discourse has been augmented by two additional modes of human knowing, giving us four main modes to contrast with the Newtonian one that was dominant for so long. The most influential is evolution, propelled into our discourse by Darwin and Spencer. Before dealing with this I note a fourth, now being reshaped by brain research, the science of consciousness, the exploration of the physiological, biochemical, or neurological core of the human condition. For many this promises to be an underpinning to all forms of human knowing, a final reconciliation between the purity of logic and the nature of Mind. For others this raises the paradox of expecting the human mind, as the apparatus that produces all knowledge, to stand outside itself and understand itself—matters that need not delay us here.

For clarity these four alternative modes of human knowing can be arranged along two dimensions—time and agency, or more specifically, given the essential subjectivity of human knowledge, human time and human agency. We can distinguish between epistemologies that presume what is to be known about is fundamentally static or universal, such as the positivistic laws of nature; time-less and true at all places. Some presume the soon-to-be-revealed laws of brain function will be of this type. Against this time-free view, we can place a dynamic view, and here evolution is the archetype. So long as we presume evolution is not toward a knowable end, mere teleology, be that perfection or equilibrium, it is a way of thinking about our engagement with the eternally dynamic as species evolve to create a new situation, so demanding further evolutionary adaptation by other species.

The evolutionary metaphor has been very productive for the social sciences and the humanities, as it has been for the life sciences, but its impact is often misunderstood. Ultimately it is about the difference between our lived time and Nature's, between the time we make and the time that is beyond our influence. The distinction above is also that between passive fatalism and engaged agency, between accepting the world as we find it and acting to change it. This distinction has been influential in European thought at least since the time of Vico, who argued for two universes of human knowledge: Nature, that which we could observe but not know fully because it was created by God, and that which we could know in quite different ways and even fully because the things known were created by us, such as our legal systems (Berlin, 2000).

Time is reinserting itself into our discourse and becoming an issue for contemporary philosophers, in the work of Bergson and Heidegger

	universal	*dynamic*
natural	positivist science	evolutionary thought
man-made	science of consciousness?	humanities' lived-time

Figure 12.2 Principal modes of human knowing.

especially. The latter distinguished between logical time, which positivist science might use, and the lived time of *Dasein*, subjective time. As we shift from the left side of the matrix to the right side, evolutionary thought is attractive because it clamps down on the inherent relativism that might otherwise render the analysis viciously circular. The selecting agent is Nature not man. But, as a result, evolutionary time must be measured in terms of species change, not in logical or lived times. Green means abandoning all notions of time that are detached from the human lived experience—such as logical or evolutionary time—and adopting a time subjectively contextualized in our life-world in terms of our life choices.

If green matters were merely about politics, there would be fewer constraints over our actions. We could discuss and agree, and modern communications means this can be amazingly rapid. Likewise we are mistaken if we think people are inherently conservative and take a long time to change their views. Even the most casual reading of the happenings during the French Revolution reminds us that people and their actions can change with terrifying speed. Green matters are especially demanding of our modes of knowing precisely because they are not only about politics and the common will; they often engage the natural world which has its own clock(s). A species' reproductive cycle constrains to our agency and the changes we might wish to make in a species' population. Breeders know this and work with it as an unchangeable time-ness that limits their agency just as the Second Law of Thermodynamics does; it sets limits to how time can be experienced in that milieu.

If the life-world-centered green discourse is indeed constrained by what man did not create (Nature), the challenge is to see how science's tremendous achievements can be brought in without pushing all other discourses aside. The power of radical doubt is that it denies science its victory. Science becomes a handmaiden to human persuasion, not its master. *Logos* is powerful but can never be determining or leave *ethos* and *pathos* behind for their interplay mirrors the human condition. Rhetoric is about persuading thinking, feeling and socialized human beings not logic engines.

It is useful to look at how Von Clausewitz argued that strategy—what we might call leadership or effective rhetorical practice—it begins when the general confronts the limits to the various actors' knowledge. But he also argued that this meant little separated from the context and practice of battle. In military terms, strategy (a) is about choosing the time and place of engagement and (b) must accompany the army into the field and reconstruct its context continuously as the battle unfolds (von Ghyczy et al., 2001). Military leadership is about the interplay of determining and adapting to the changing context of action. While this pushes the general's agency to the fore, denying any scientific model or theory priority, science can provide some powerful and rigorous language for defining the context and communicating the leader's intentions. We can plot the enemy positions and tell our troops to advance out of their line of fire. We can use the Second Law to calculate the heat losses and energy demands of various action options. Science, along with the relevant social, legal and psychological constraints that lie beyond the rhetor's influence, helps describe the context of action without determining the general's choices. It helps outline the socio-political context into which human agency is projected— what we might call the solution space. That space is the lived-world and cannot ever be defined by science alone. Clearly science is essential to the green discourse, helping define some options, but its hegemonic impulses must be restrained and held subservient to the life-world and its own lived time. As leaders make green proposals, they engage human audiences with deep intuitions about how time works in their lives. Lived time is remarkably fluid and changeable while logical and evolutionary times are not. Thus, rhetoric is often regarded as the activity of making others aware of possibilities they had not previously refracted into their everyday living. A rhetor's ability to frame green issues is constrained by these experience-based time and space intuitions for they are, by definition, in the audience's lived world, one far from the laboratory or the library.

Overall this chapter argues green issues cannot to be considered objectively in the ways normally implied by the scientific committees and experts as they pontificate or as natural experiments to be conducted by governments or corporations. Those affected lie outside these constellations of power and must seize the conversation. Green matters' difficulty lies precisely in the fact they are lived and are inherently political. Stakeholder theory, workable or not, is likewise inherently green because it is about negotiating the distribution of burdens and benefits among the people involved. Corporations have no capability to be green beyond their stakeholders' actions, and are seldom open to what all of them have to say either. The bottom line is that green is not merely intellectual, academically interesting and demanding as it might seem. Thinking productively about it cannot be disengaged from the political, social and economic realities of our life-world. Green demands, on the one hand, a new appreciation of the limits of scientific thinking and, on the other, an appreciation of the limits to political and economic possibility. To pretend otherwise is to put off the post-modern realization that we are being challenged to think beyond technological fixes to the problems that our technologies have created, beyond transferring green problems to those claiming scientific analysis is power, and conclude that green presupposes making our species' collective experience and expectation central to the discourse. This might move us onward from the academic elitism of Enlightenment thinking to a green humanist conversation before it is too late, before our lived time runs out. Doing so might open up a new universe of life-world-centered ethics and morality that could take us back to the animism of previous pre-scientific or pre-modern civilizations.

REFERENCES

Berlin, I. (2000). *Three critics of the enlightenment: Vico, Hamann, Herder.* Princeton, NJ: Princeton University Press.

Conley, T. M. (1990). *Rhetoric in the European tradition.* Chicago: University of Chicago Press.

Gore, A. (1993). *Earth in the balance: Ecology and the human spirit.* New York: Plume.

Gutas, D. (1998), *Greek thought, Arab culture: The GraecoArabic translation movement in Baghdad and Early Abbasid society (2nd–4th/8th–10th centuries).* Abingdon Oxon: Routledge.

Huntington, S. P. (2003). *The clash of civilizations and the remaking of world order,* New York: Simon & Schuster.

Popper, K. R. (1945). *The open society and its enemies.* London: Routledge.

———(1969). *Conjectures and refutations: The growth of scientific knowledge* (3rd ed.). London: Routledge and Kegan Paul.

Ryle, G. (1954). *Dilemmas: The Tarner lectures, 1953.* Cambridge: Cambridge University Press.

Simon, H. A. (1981). *The sciences of the artificial* (2nd ed.). Cambridge, MA: MIT Press.

Snow, C. P. (1959). *The two cultures and the scientific revolution: The Rede lecture 1959.* Cambridge: Cambridge University Press.

von Ghyczy, T., von Oetinger, B., & Bassford, C. (Eds.) (2001). *Clausewitz on strategy: Inspiration and insight from a master strategist.* New York: John Wiley & Sons.

Contributors

Elizabeth Anastasi is Economic Adviser, Low-Carbon and Sustainable Development at the Department for Business, Innovation and Skills. Anastasi graduated from the London School of Economics in 2004 after studying for a B.Sc. in economics and joined the former Department of Trade and Industry as part of the economist Faststream. After completing a Masters in Economics at the Sorbonne in Paris, she rejoined the former Department for Business, Enterprise and Regulatory Reform in September 2008 as an economic adviser working on low-carbon business opportunities and sustainable development. In particular, she worked on the economic evidence supporting the recently published Low-Carbon Industrial Strategy. Liz continues to work as an Economic Advisor within the low-carbon and sustainable area for the Department for Business, Innovation and Skills. She also recently completed a part-time secondment to the Committee on Climate Change as part of the team working on a review of low-carbon innovation in the UK.

Richard Broyd is a Partner of the Monitor Group based in London. Prior to this, Broyd was chief executive of a substantial family office; held a number of positions at Montedison, including managing director of a specialty chemical company and director of strategy and control; was regional manager for an international economic consultancy advising governments and major corporations as well as publishing extensive reports on economic prospects for many countries and industries. In 1980 he was awarded a Ph.D. in regional economic development by Cornell University and was at the United Nations Center for Regional Development, Nagoya, Japan. Richard has served as chairman and board member of several private and public companies and is currently a director of Sollers in Moscow, a major European family office and chairman of Reach to Teach, a charity.

Jeff Grogan is a senior partner at Monitor Group and a leader in the firm's national economic development and security practice. He advises business and government leaders on issues concerning national, regional and cluster competitiveness. While directing competitiveness projects and providing advice to Monitor clients and colleagues worldwide, he oversees the development and commercialization of new competitiveness applications and tools. Grogan has led numerous national, regional and cluster competitiveness studies in the United States. He directed a multi-region, multi-cluster competitiveness project, the *United States Clusters of Innovation Initiative*, as well as regional and cluster competitiveness projects across the United States. He led a study to profile the economic performance and competitiveness of the United States for the nation's governors and briefed them on the study results. He has served on presidential and gubernatorial transition teams addressing topics of national and regional competitiveness. Jeff is also actively engaged with Monitor colleagues and clients in economic competitiveness projects in Europe, Asia and the Middle East. He directed a multinational initiative to benchmark and recommend policies to advance entrepreneurship. He directed an effort to develop a proprietary database of advanced critical infrastructure security-related technologies for use by both public and private sector clients. Grogan has also developed corporate and business unit strategies for clients in industries including defense electronics, automotive products, steel, shipbuilding, telecommunications and professional services.

Prior to joining Monitor Group, Grogan served as an officer in the United States Navy. He was the navigator and gunnery officer of a guided missile destroyer. He served as combat systems officer on the battle staff of a destroyer squadron commander and as a tactical action officer for warfare commanders in aircraft carrier battle group contingency operations in the Pacific and Indian Oceans and the Arabian Sea.

Grogan is a director of the Massachusetts Technology Collaborative, MassInc and the Fitzie Foundation. He is a member of the board of governors of the John Adams Innovation Institute. He is a trustee of Noble and Greenough School, and Tenacre Country Day School. Grogan received his Master of Business Administration degree in 1987 from the University of Virginia's Darden Graduate School of Business Administration, and a Bachelor of Science degree in International Security Affairs in 1978 from the United States Naval Academy.

Alejandro Gutierrez is an architect and Associate Director at Arup Urban Design leading a range of urban development projects globally such as Dongtan Eco City–Shanghai, Wanzhuang Eco City–Beijing, Dubai Waterfront Masterplan Sustainability Review and the competition brief for Copenhagen Port Regeneration Strategy. He joined Arup in 2002.

In addition, he is an invited lecturer to UCL Bartlett School of Architecture, London School of Economics, Universidad Iberoamericana in Mexico and Universidad Catolica in Chile.

Prior to joining Arup he was director for Cities Consultancy Unit at Catholic University in Santiago, Chile, and also director for Cities and Environment area at the Architecture School in the same university where he was advisor to the minister of housing and urbanism on specific urban projects.

Noreena Hertz is Duisenberg Professor of Globalization, Sustainability and Finance based at both the Rotterdam School of Management, Erasmus University and the University of Cambridge. Hertz's work offers a much needed blueprint for rethinking economics. Her unique, integrated approach weaves traditional economic analysis into foreign policy trends, psychology and sociology. Hertz's career began in St. Petersburg where she completed her MBA at Wharton and helped establish the city's stock exchange. Hertz then became a consultant at the World Bank, advising the Russian government on economic reforms, specifically the shift from a communist model to a capitalist system. After gaining her Ph.D. at Cambridge, Hertz moved to the Middle East, where she headed a team of 40 researchers exploring potential roles for the private sector in the peace process.

In her number one best-selling book *The Silent Takeover*, Hertz predicted that unregulated markets and massive financial institutions would have serious global consequences. This prescience has lead to many describing Professor Hertz as a visionary. Her 2005 best seller, *The Debt Threat: How Debt Is Destroying the Developing World . . . and Threatening Us All*, exposed the dangers of irrational lending. Hertz played a leading role in the development of (RED) an innovative commercial model to raise money for AIDS victims in Africa having inspired Bono (co-founder of the project) with her writings. Hertz's op-ed pieces have been published in several key publications including *The Washington Post* and *The Financial Times*. Alongside a heavy broadcasting and writing schedule, Hertz regularly participates in debates and panel discussions with leading politicians and public figures. She also advises major multinational corporations, CEOs, NGOs and start-up companies and sits on various corporate and charitable Boards.

Edward Hyams is a Partner in Englefield Capital having first met their investment partners to work on the Zephyr renewables transaction in 2003 and works mainly on energy, environmental and infrastructure investments at Englefield. Hyams is non-executive chairman of the UK Energy Saving Trust (www.est.org.uk), taking up this role in April 2005 as a result of a long-standing interest and experience in energy efficiency and sustainability. He also chairs a UK energy and infrastructure "think tank"—the Utility Strategy Group.

While managing director at Eastern Group (Eastern Electricity) in the late 1990, he was founder chairman of the East of England Round Table for Sustainable Development and has participated in numerous national policy groups on energy, the environment and sustainability. He was named UK Best Business Leader in the 2002 Sage Daily Telegraph Business awards as CEO of a new UK Energy Business. Hyams is a chartered engineer with a degree in electrical engineering from Imperial College and has a post-graduate qualification in accounting and finance.

Jack Keenan is the founder and CEO of Grand Cru Consulting Ltd. He has been chairman and CEO of Kraft Foods International, and CEO of the business which is now Diageo plc. Keenan has served as an executive director on the Diageo and Moet Hennessey boards, and as a non-executive on the boards of Marks & Spencer plc, Tomkins plc, The Body Shop International and General Mills, Inc. He is a director of National Angels Ltd.—a theatre production company that has produced *History Boys* and *War Horse* in the West End together with the National Theatre. Keenan has been patron of the Centre for International Business & Management at Judge Business School for eight years. The principal clients of Grand Cru Consulting are today Oaktree Capital Management, the Stock Spirits Group SARL (which he chairs) and Revolymer Ltd. He graduated from Tufts University with honors and has an MBA from Harvard. He is a resident of the United Kingdom.

Debra Lam is a Senior Policy Consultant at Arup with experience in governance, sustainable development, socially responsible investments and project management. Lam works across a broad span of sectors, from non-profit organizations to federal and local governments. Her ongoing research and analysis includes low-carbon strategies for new builds and retrofits, climate change adaptation and mitigation and the resilience of cities to combat climate change and transition to a low-carbon economy. Lam received her undergraduate degree in Foreign Service at Georgetown University and her graduate degree in public policy at the University of California, Berkeley. She is an LEED Accredited Professional.

Michael Littlechild is a Founder-Director of GoodCorporation and leads the delivery of its ethical assessment services. He is a former partner of KPMG Consulting in the Strategic Business Management group which served KPMG's leading clients. At GoodCorporation he has led teams to undertake ethical assessments which review policies and working processes to analyze how businesses comply with their declared ethical policies. He has extensive experience in Europe, the Middle East, Africa, the United States, China and Southeast Asia. He also leads GoodCorporation's anti-bribery and corruption services. Michael was formerly a research fellow at the European Policy Research Center at the University of Strathclyde and is on the Advisory Board of the International Center for Corporate Social Responsibility at Nottingham Business School. He is a trustee of Awards for Young Musicians.

Alexandra Mandelbaum is a Consultant based in Monitor's New York office. She has worked on developing corporate strategies for clients in various industries, including pharmaceuticals, pulp and paper industries, governments and educational institutions. She has worked for clients in Brazil, most of Latin America, Russia and the United States. Recent client engagements have included the development of a comprehensive five-year strategic plan for a pharmaceutical company for the Latin American Region; the development of the positioning and strategy for a Russian university; the facilitation of a series of workshops for seven U.S. state governments to develop statewide economic strategies and mechanisms for implementation; the creation of several non-profit entities' five-year growth strategy plans; scenario analysis on the future of Cuba; extensive content development for a series of training sessions and executive off-sites for Monitor's Regional Competitiveness practice; and the management of a year-long project focused on mapping and expanding the reach of market-based solutions to poverty in Africa.

Prior to joining Monitor, she worked as an emerging markets equity research analyst for JP Morgan Chase, with a specialization in the steel sector. Prior to that, she was the assistant to Spanish High Court Judge Baltasar Garzón on a project of counterterrorism cooperation between Europe and the United States, as well as a university instructor. Mandelbaum has a Ph.D. from New York University, an M.Phil. from Cambridge University, and a B.A. from Harvard University. She grew up in Spain and is fluent in five languages.

Christos Pitelis is Director of the Center for International Business and Management (CIBAM) and reader in International Business and Competitiveness at the Judge Business School, as well as a Fellow in Economics at Queens' College, University of Cambridge. Christos has published extensively in scholarly journals such as *Organization Science, Journal of International Business Studies, Organization Studies, International Journal of Industrial Organization, Management International Review* and *Industrial and Corporate Change*. He is the editor of the *Collected Papers of Edith Penrose*, on the editorial boards of *Organization Science, Organization Studies* and *Management International Review* and a guest editor for *Organization Studies, Corporate Governance, International Business Review, Management International Review* and *Industrial and Corporate Change* (on the theory of the firm, globalization, international business, regulation, global governance and global finance). Christos has researched, consulted and co-ordinated projects for many governments, the European Commission, the United Nations, USAID, the Commonwealth Secretariat, and the private sector. He has been visiting professor in Europe, Russia, China, Latin America and the United States (for example, Berkeley, Copenhagen Business School,

MIT, China-Europe Management Institute, University of St. Petersburg). Since 1999 he is included in the Marquis *Who's Who in the World.*

Michael Pollitt is a University Reader in business economics at the Judge Business School, University of Cambridge and director of studies in economics and management at Sidney Sussex College, Cambridge. He is an assistant director of the ESRC Electricity Policy Research Group. In 2007 he was appointed as external economic advisor to Ofgem, the UK's energy regulator. Since early 2008 he has been a member of the New Zealand Commerce Commission's expert panel on input methodologies for the regulation of electricity, gas and airports. He has been convenor of the Association of Christian Economists UK since 2000.

Pollitt holds a BA in economics from Cambridge and an M.Phil. and a D.Phil. in economics from Oxford. He has been a fellow of Sidney Sussex since 1994. On business ethics, he works with Ian Jones (Center for Business Research, Cambridge) and is the co-author (with Ian) of *Multinationals in Their Communities: A Social Capital Approach to Corporate Citizenship Projects* (Palgrave, 2007) and co-editor of *The Role of Business Ethics in Economic Performance* (Macmillan, 1998) and *Understanding How Ethical Issues Develop* (Palgrave, 2002).

Vicky Pryce is a Senior Managing Director in FTI's Economic Consulting practice, and is based in the London office. Vicky joined FTI in September 2010 and leads on business economics, working with leading companies on issues from corporate strategy to public policy. Prior to this, she was Director General, Economics & Chief Economic Adviser, Department for Business, Innovation and Skills (BIS), 2002-2010 and Joint Head, UK Government Economic Service, 2007-2010. Vicky is a member of the Secretary of State for Business Panel on monitoring the economy and also a member of Vince Cable's Business Advisory Group.

Before joining the civil service Vicky was Partner at London Economics, Partner and Chief Economist at KPMG, Corporate Economist at Esso Europe and Chief Economist at Williams & Glyn's Bank (later RBS). She was also instrumental in the creation of GoodCorporation, a company formed to promote Corporate Social Responsibility.

Vicky is a visiting Professor at the CASS Business School, a fellow of the Society of Business Economists, Adjunct Professor at Imperial College Business School and a visiting Fellow at Nuffield College, Oxford. She is on the Council at the University of Kent and on the Advisory Board for the Centre for International Business and Management (CIBAM) at the Judge Institute at Cambridge University. She is also a member of the Standing Advisory Group of the Financial Reporting Review Panel (FRRP), and of the International Advisory Board of British American Business Inc (BABI). She serves as a Fellow at the RSA and a Freeman and Liveryman at the City of London and has just become the first female Master of the Worshipful Company of Management Consultants. She is also on the Board of Trustees at the Centre for Economic Policy Research (CEPR) and Patron of "Pro-Bono" Economics.

David Roth is CEO of The Store–WPP (Europe, Middle East, Africa and Asia). Roth started his career at the House of Commons working for a Member of Parliament. He swapped the cut and thrust of politics for the cut and thrust of advertising. He joined Bates Dorland as a strategic planner becoming main board director for strategy and the managing director of the consulting and digital divisions. Roth led the worldwide retail and technology center of excellence for the international agency group. After working as a management consultant, Roth joined Kingfisher's B&Q plc one of Europe's largest retailers sitting on the main board of directors as UK and international marketing director. In 2008 he joined WPP as the CEO of The Store–WPP Global Retail Practice for EMEA and Asia. A frequent keynote speaker, international lecturer and author, he is also the host of *The Store TV* an on-line retailing magazine program. Roth is a non-executive director of TFT the Geneva-based NGO which specializes in supply chain best practices that are socially responsible and protect the environment.

Jochen Runde is Director of the MBA program at Judge Business School. He is co-editor of the *Cambridge Journal of Economics* and a member of the Cambridge Social Ontology Group (CSOG) and the Centre for Process Excellence and Innovation. He is a former Fellow of the Cambridge-MIT Institute (CMI), where he served as associate director of the Professional Practice Program (2001–2003) and director of Graduate Programs (2003–2005). He has also served as director of Programs at Judge Business School (2007–2008), on the Cambridge University Board of Graduate Studies (2003–2008), and as an author and consultant to Interactyx, a company that produces interactive electronic books, digital media players and course management systems. Jochen has taught at Judge Business School since 1999, prior to which he was a fellow and lecturer in economics (1992–1999) and Doris Woodall Research Fellow (1991–1992) at Girton College, Cambridge. Before moving to Cambridge, Jochen taught at the Department of Economics, University of the Witwatersrand, in Johannesburg (1984–1990). His research interests include the development and commercialization of digital technologies; the philosophy of economics and the social sciences more widely; social ontology; probability, uncertainty and rational choice theory; Austrian economics and the economics of institutions.

J. C. Spender is currently Svenska Handelsbanken Visiting Professor at the School of Economics and Management, Lund University (Sweden) and Visiting Professor ESADE/Universitat Ramon Llull (Spain). He is also visiting at Open University Business School, Cranfield School of Management, Leeds University Business School and the International School of Management (Paris). He retired from full-time employment in 2003.

Spender obtained a B.A. and M.A. in Engineering from Oxford University, followed by a Ph.D. in Corporate Strategy from Manchester Business School. Prior to Oxford, he served in RN experimental submarines. On graduation he joined Rolls Royce & Associates to do reactor design and development work on the UK nuclear submarine program. He then moved to IBM as large account salesman and team leader, followed by strategy consulting. He then pursued a career in investment banking, but left to enter the Manchester Ph.D. program. His thesis was awarded the U.S. Academy of Management AT Kearney Prize in 1980, published as *Industry Recipes* (Blackwell, 1989). Spender has served on the faculties of City University (London), York University (Toronto), UCLA, University of Glasgow, and occupied the Chair of Entrepreneurship and Small Business at Rutgers (State University of New Jersey). After a year's sabbatical with the Advanced Technology Program (U.S. Department of Commerce), he was appointed dean of the School of Management, New York Institute of Technology and later dean of the School of Business and Technology, Fashion Institute of Technology (SUNY), New York.

Sir Crispin Tickell is Director of the Policy Foresight Programme, James Martin 21st Century School at Oxford University. Most of his career was in the Diplomatic Service. He was Chef de Cabinet to the President of the European Commission (1977–1980), Ambassador to Mexico (1981–1983), Permanent Secretary of the Overseas Development Administration (1984–1987), British Permanent Representative to the United Nations (1987–1990), and Warden of Green College, Oxford (1990–1997). He is an author and contributor to many publications on environmental, climate and related issues.

Index